Glorious Gardens of Cornwall

Edited by
SUE PRING

with a Foreword by
ROY LANCASTER

The Cornwall Gardens Trust

Cornwall Gardens Trust would like to thank the Countryside Commission, the Rural Development Commission and Devon and Cornwall Training and Enterprise Council. without whose generous support and financial backing the production of this book would not have been possible.

The Trust is especially grateful to Tim Smit of Heligan for his enthusiasm and backing, and to the private garden owners and others such as the National Trust, other charities and local authorities, for allowing details of their gardens to be published by Cornwall Gardens Trust and for their personal contributions to this book.

First published in Great Britain 1996
by Cornwall Gardens Trust

© 1996 Cornwall Gardens Trust

ISBN 0 9528984 0 3

Designed and produced by Production Line, Oxford
Printed in Great Britain by Bath Colourbooks, Glasgow

Contents

Arum lilies *(Zantedeschia aethiopica)* at Trebah

Foreword

I can't explain why, but just as I get more excited about travelling east when leaving Britain, it has always been the reverse when leaving my home in Hampshire, for a destination in this country. Perhaps it is the fact that the west, and the south-west in particular, is (or used to be) wetter and its plant life more lush than in eastern Britain; or maybe it is the traditionally milder climate that beckons. In truth, it is undoubtedly a mixture of both these factors, which have resulted in some of the most satisfying and exciting gardens in a country renowned worldwide for its variety of ornamental cultivation. I speak, of course, principally as a plantsman and plant explorer, for it is in this role that I first visited Cornwall 30 years ago – and I was not disappointed.

In Cornwall there are gardens old and young, neglected, rescued and still in the making. In them grow plants from the far corners of the earth – magnolias from the Himalaya, camellias from Japan, fire trees from the Andes and strange things from the Antipodes, in surroundings as alien to them as their native habitats are to us. Despite this, however, they flourish as if in paradise, cocooned oftentimes in lush hedges that temper the wind.

I have yet to see a list of all the plants at present cultivated out of doors in Cornwall; were such a list available I should not be surprised to see it representing all the continents and most of the countries of the temperate world. For 200 years or more, plant hunters have found the warm toe of Britain a suitable home for their most treasured collections and today's visitors can gaze upon camellias, pieris, rhododendrons, conifers and a thousand and one other plants introduced by these intrepid explorers and adventurers.

Not only are the gardens of Cornwall a reminder to us of the world's natural gardens and their exotic vegetation, they are also showcases for the hybridising skills of many of its gardeners, who have taken the wild species introduced from afar to breed new garden plants as diverse as camellias and daffodils. Few other, if any, other counties can boast such plant diversity as is found in the gardens described in this book, and I warmly commend it to all those visiting Cornwall whether for the first or the umpteenth time.

Roy Lancaster

Carew's Fishful Pond at Antony

Introduction

One of the great pleasures of living in or visiting Cornwall is having the opportunity to visit such a wide variety of gardens. These range from small intimate gardens at the beginning of their creation to the ancient splendour and complex layouts of the grand estates.

The aim of this book is to provide a descriptive background to all the gardens, both public and private, that are open to the public on a regular basis and also to give a concise introduction to the history and horticultural specialities of the county.

Gardens included are the the majority of those to be found in the Annual Gardens Open Guide (produced by the Cornwall Gardens Society and the Cornwall Tourist Board) which should be consulted for specific opening times, where these vary from year to year. If in doubt, visitors are asked to telephone in advance.

Thanks are due to the garden owners for their contributions, and also all those who supplied background information

I should like to acknowledge the assistance of the following people without whom the production of this book would not have been possible: Tim Smit (whose 'inspired' idea it was in the first place); the Committee members of the CGT for their encouragement and assistance; Mike Bell and Nigel Holman for their respective contributions; Stuart Harding (Countryside Commission), George Musgrove and John Bareham (RDC), and Malcolm Bell (Devon and Cornwall Training and Enterprise Council) for their decision to assist in funding; Charlie Webster for producing a well laid out publication; Meriel Thurston for her sterling efforts in translating my scribbles; the staff of the RIC and CRO; and most importantly all the garden owners whose hard work and dedication have created so many lovely gardens.

Sue Pring

ABBREVIATIONS USED

NT: National Trust
RIC: Royal Institute of Cornwall
CRO: Cornwall Record Office

PICTURE CREDITS

I would like to thank the following for providing photographs and for permission to use copyright material. Whilst every effort has been to trace and acknowledge copyright holders, I apologise for any omissions.
Back cover - CTB, Front cover - C. Matthews, 2 - S Pring, 4 - NT/D Flunder, 8 - M Schofield, 12 - NT, 13 - C Wetherhill, 14 - CAU/S Hartgroves, 15 - NT, 16 top - British Library, 16 bottom - RIC, 17 - CAU & Prideaux-Brune family, 18 top - RIC, 18 - Mount Edgcumbe, 19 - NT/D Flunder, 19 - N Mathews, 20 top - CRO GHW 1a & lb, 20 - CRO G 1957, 21 - F W L Stockdale, 23 - T Hudson, 23 bottom - S Pring, 24 - T Hudson, 25 - Prideaux-Brune family, 26 - J D Sedding, 27 - N Mathews, 28 - S Pring, 29 - CRO DCPenwith 814,

PLANTS AND PLANTING
30 - NT/J Gifford, 31 - B Candy, 32 - C Matthews, 33 - C Matthews, 35 - S Pring, 36 - Penzance Public Library

MAGNOLIAS, RHODODENDRONS AND CAMELLIAS
37 - C Matthews, 38 top - S Pring, 38 bottom - C Matthews, 39 top - Trewithen Estates, 39 bottom - Heligan Gardens, 40 - S Pring, 41 - CTB/J Becker

FRUIT
44 top - RIC, 44 bottom - C Matthews, 45 top - RIC, 45 bottom - J Evans, 46 top - S Pring, 47 - English Nature, 47 - S Pring, 48 - C Matthews

HORTICULTURE
42 top - RIC, 49 - RIC, 50 top - C Matthews, 50 - Penzance Library

GAZETTEER
51 - NT/W Fox, 52 - NT/D Flunder, 53 - The Tate Gallery, 54 - Boconnoc Estate, 55 - M Perry, 56 - A Dance, 57 - S Slaughter, 58 - N Mathews, 60 - N Mathews, 61 - J Wilks,

62 - C Matthews, 64 - NT/A Besley, 65 - S Pring, 66 - S Pring, 67 - S Pring, 68 - C Matthews, 70 - NT/T Lintell, 71 - NT/C Fox, 72 - M Schofield, 73 - J Hill, 75 - C Matthews, 75 - Heligan Gardens, 77 top - J C Mann, 77 bottom - S Pring, 78 top - N Mathews, 78 bottom - K R Willcock, 79 - M Brent, 80 - M Brent, 81 - R Gilbert, 82 - NT/A Besley, 84 - D Crawford, 85 - S Pring, 86 - M Campbell-Culver, 87 - A Drew Whurr, 89 - C Matthews, 90 - N Mathews, 91 - R Morin, 92 - T F Ellis, 94 - NT/A Besley, 96 - S Clemo, 98 - S Pring, 99 - CTB, 100 - N Mathews, 101 top & bottom - C Matthews, 103 - Beric Tempest Ltd, 104 - NT/J P Godeaut, 105 top - C Matthews, 105 bottom - S Pring, 106 - CTB, 107 - CTB/J Becker, 108 - S Pring, 109 - C Matthews, 110 - C Matthews, 111 - Sir F Vyvyan, 112 - NT/T Lintell, 113 - NT/T Lintell, 115 - M Nelhams, 116 - Trevarno Enterprises, 117 - M Snellgrove, 118 - Trewithen Estate, 119 - C Matthews, 120 - S Pring, 122 - CRO BTru 271, 123 - N & M Froggatt

Cornwall Gardens Trust Garden Records

- Bareppa House, Mawnan Smith
- Barbara Hepworth Museum & Sculpture Garden, St Ives
- Bochym, Nr. Helston
- Bosahan, St. Anthony-in-Meneage
- Bosvigo House, Truro
- Burncoose, Gwennap
- Carwinion, Mawnan Smith
- Catchfrench, St Germans • II*
- Carclew, Perran-ar-Worthal • II
- Clowance, Crowan
- Enys, St. Gluvias • II
- Ethy House, St. Winnow
- Fox Rosehill, Falmouth
- Gyllyngdune Garden, Falmouth
- Godolphin, Breage
- Killiow, Kea
- Lis Escop, Feock
- Lismore, Helston • II
- Morrab Gardens, Penzance
- Menehay, Budock
- Meudon Hotel, Mawnan Smith
- Pengersick Castle, Germoe
- Pengreep, Gwennap

- Penjerrick, Mawnan Smith
- Penlee Memorial Garden, Penzance
- Prideaux Place, Padstow • II
- Pine Lodge, Cuddra, St. Austell
- Port Eliot, St. Germans • I
- Scorrier, Redruth
- St. Michael's Mount • II
- The Downes, Hayle • II
- Trebah, Mawnan Smith • II
- The Hollies, Grampound
- Tregullow, Redruth
- Trereife, Penzance
- Trelowarren, Helston • II
- Trevarno, Sithney • II
- Trewidden, Penzance
- Treworgan, Mawnan Smith
- Triste House, Veryan
- Wellesley House, Saltash
- Wetherham, St. Tudy
- Whiteford, Stoke Climsland

I, II* and II denote a garden listed and graded by English Heritage

The gate at Godolphin by Elmer Schofield

Cornwall Gardens Trust

Cornwall Gardens Trust was formed in 1988 "to preserve, enhance and re-create whatever garden land may exist or have existed in Cornwall". The gardens of Cornwall are a unique heritage ranging from the early gardens of prehistoric settlements through the golden age of gardening in the eighteenth and nineteenth centuries to the present day, the mild climate making Cornwall truly the garden county of England.

The Trust is thoroughly practical: teams of Recorders are assembling an archival record of the gardens and parkland in Cornwall. These records gather together knowledge of a particular garden and at the same time extend knowledge of gardening in the county. They also draw attention to the gardens' particular features, both for the owners and for the local and national authorities. Although most owners know a good deal about their gardens, surprises are sometimes uncovered and if, for instance, properties change hands, the Garden Record becomes very important.

A wide range of gardens has so far been recorded, the most modern being Pine Lodge near St Austell and the oldest, an Elizabethan garden, at Godolphin House, Breage. As the overall archive develops, knowledge increases regarding garden development within the county and also the links between gardens.

A Garden Record is made when an interested owner asks for one, English Heritage requests one, or the Trust seeks permission to make one, and they are in such demand that there is a waiting list for them. The Record can be the first step to getting a garden listed on the English Heritage Register of Historic Parks and Gardens, which brings considerable advantages. Although not every garden is worthy of listing, and some owners do not want such listing, a number of gardens in Cornwall are of national importance and all are important within the county. If some particularly interesting feature is noted during recording, the Trust can (with the owner's permission) forward a copy of the Record to English Heritage and the Countryside Commission. Following on from this, if the Record justifies it, the Countryside Commission has, up to now, provided a grant towards the production of a management plan by consultants which can be a great help to the owner; listing can follow, which opens up the possibility of grant aid for restoration. The Trust has been instrumental in assisting a number of Cornish garden owners in this way.

The C.G.T. Council of Management has members who are owners of gardens such as Antony, Chyverton, Heligan and Trebah, together with people from like-minded organisations such as the National Trust and the N.C.C.P.G., and the Trust membership covers many owners of gardens both great and small which are important in their Cornish context. Specialist members of the Trust offer expert advice in analysing garden design, suggesting overall management plans or how to deal with particular restoration problems.

From the Garden Record it is possible to identify projects which the Trust can assist both practically and financially. A Small Grant Scheme is available for approved garden projects and the Trust will assist in seeking funding for larger projects, as for example at Prideaux in Padstow where the Victorian sunken garden was restored with the help of the Trust.

The gardens of Cornwall are a very important part of the county and national heritage and are visited by many thousands of people every year; Cornwall Gardens Trust records the gardens past and present and fosters their future, publishing an annual Journal and Newsletter with an interesting programme of visits to gardens that are seldom open. New members are always welcome.

Daphne Lawry MBE –Secretary.

Map by Sue Pring

Location Map

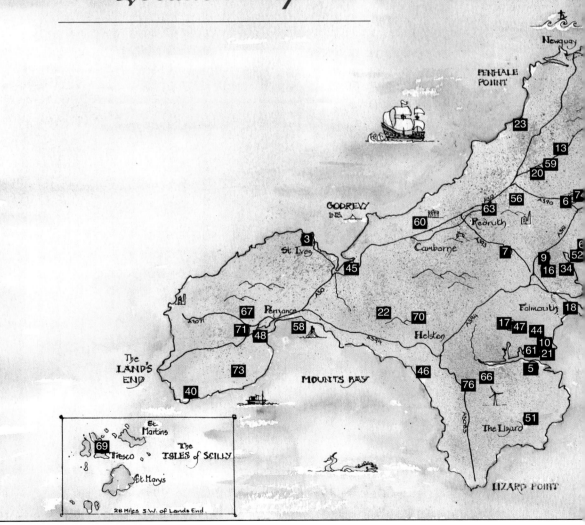

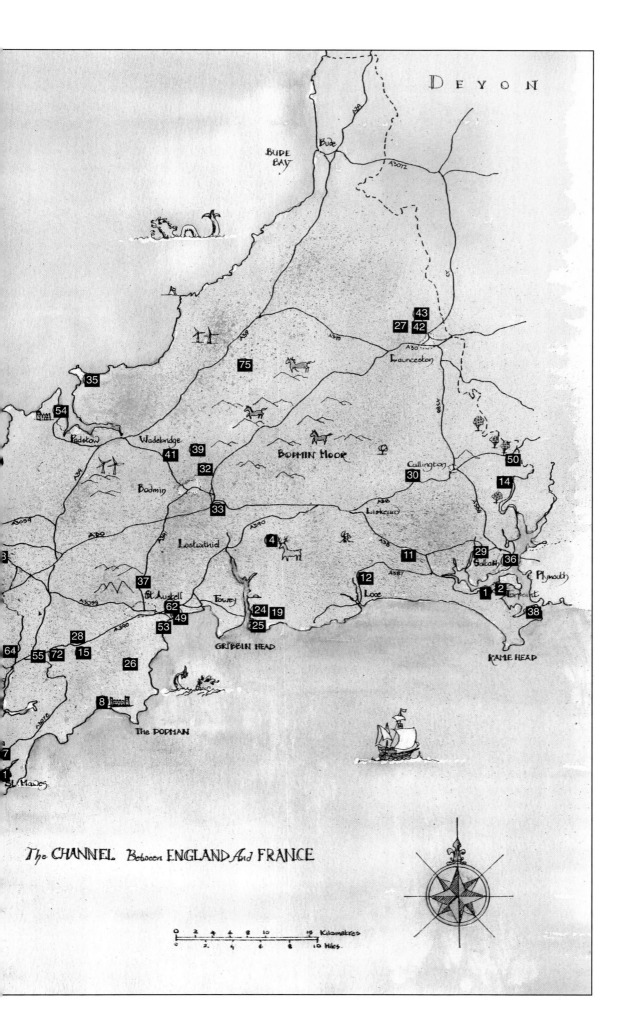

The CHANNEL Between ENGLAND And FRANCE

The coast at Predannack

Historical Background

Cornwall is an old land, old beyond imagining – the echoes of ancient times affect most of those who live here and many others who are drawn to the West for their relaxation. In the granite uplands of central Cornwall are to be seen the remains of the tremendous Armorican mountain ranges of 240 million years ago, worn down throughout the ages to become the rounded moorland hummocks forming the central spine of the county.

More recently, after the last Ice Age, only (!) eight thousand years ago, the drowned river valleys typical of southern Cornwall were formed by the sea flooding up the valleys following the melting of the ice caps. The presence of water is all pervading still – Cornwall is surrounded on three sides by the sea and is the first landfall for the moisture laden westerly winds to shed their burden. This moisture gives the county its character and reputation; not just for rainfall, but also for an extraordinary quality of light. The watery atmosphere creates special conditions beloved by artists and also provides an almost tropical level of humidity which has become the perfect environment for both native and introduced plantings.

Gardens

"In the beginning"

The first gardens of Cornwall were in all probability made during Neolithic times (2,500 BC) around the settlements of small round huts such as those found at Carn Brea near Camborne. In nearby plots surrounding the settlement the inhabitants would have tilled the ground with stone hoes, deer horn picks and primitive ploughs made of animals' shoulder blades. Although discoveries of this way of life are the prerogative of archaeologists, we may still see the remnants of the gardens of a later culture at Chysauster in the far west.

This well documented site, thought to date from the Romano-British period (100 BC - 300 AD), is composed of a cluster of courtyard houses with adjacent garden plots and small terraced fields. Although ploughs were used on the largest fields, the smaller plots would have been dug by hand. Impressions of the triangular ended spade (still used today and known as the Cornish shovel) have been found on sites of this period.

Aerial photograph of the Roman-British settlement at Chysauster

Plants known to have been grown and which are easily identified include the cereals: emmer wheat, spelt wheat and barley. Other plants whose remains are often difficult to identify, such as onions and leeks and an early form of carrot and parsnip, may also have been grown. The coastal areas would have provided a source of wild examples of plants such as sea beet and wild carrot which may have been taken into the fields for protection and improvement. Seed remains of brambles, wild apples and sloes have also been found — it is probable that the first domestication of the apple may have been started by choosing particularly large specimens of the wild fruit and propagating them in the enclosed garden plots.

The only known Roman villa in Cornwall was at Magor near Camborne. Here, although very little was discovered, an interesting aspect giving some light on the artistic traditions linked with plants can be seen in the decoration used – an area of plaster from the wall was painted with tulip or lotus buds.

The small-scale fields associated with this period were used throughout the following centuries (the so-called Dark Ages) for which there is no horticultural information.

The holy men who first came to Cornwall in the 5th and 6th centuries did not build large monasteries but had small unsophisticated hermitages or cells, at best a cluster of huts around a tiny church. It was not until the 12th and 13th centuries that larger monastic establishments came into being – Benedictine priories being founded at Tywardreath and Glasney near Penryn. These had much more complicated and extensive gardens to provide both food and medicinal herbs for the monks. Orchards, too, were planted and, thanks to the extensive communication with Brittany and northern Europe, plants and seeds exchanged. Vineyards were laid out and plants such as saffron grown. (Still existing are a number of associated field names such as Saffron Meadow at Penryn.)

Many castles were also built at this time and they too had gardens for both food and pleasure. A rare survival of this period is to be found at the famous and legendary site of Tintagel – although an exposed site for gardening, it nevertheless contained a small walled garden which would have mitigated the effect of the elements.

Although there are no actual garden features still existing on the site, apart from perimeter cross paths and remnants of slate edged beds, illustrations and documentary sources of sites of the same period elsewhere can give a good indication of the likely lay-out. In more sheltered sites fruit trees were usually present together with lawns studded with wild flowers and raised turf benches. Water features such as pools and fountains were also

Remains of the medieval garden at Tintagel (the garden is the small square on the island)

common, as were railings and trellises with climbing plants such as roses and honeysuckle. It has been suggested that, due to the infrequent visits of royalty to the castle, a form of "bedding out" was practised, with plants brought in only when a visit was due!

It was also during the Middle Ages that a number of deer parks were laid out. These were a Royal prerogative, extended to the Church and notable families. In 1258, the Bishop of Exeter was granted the right to "impale" deer at a number of his Cornish manors including Glasney and Lanner. Many of these parks were abandoned by the mid-15th century and most others by the 16th century, and today the only surviving early deer park is at Boconnoc.

Although there are no known examples of gardens from this time, there are many indications that ornamental plants and flowers were well known. This can be demonstrated in church architecture, where wonderful stone and wood carvings depict all kinds of plants ranging from the well-known oak and rose to the more exotic grape vine.

Gardens were small 'herbers' similar to the monks' gardens, and as early as 1444 a neighbourhood dispute about a weedy garden resulted in a certain John Cary of Mitchell being fined for leaving his field and garden fallow – to the hurt of his neighbours. (Today the small village of Mitchell still has remnants of its strip field systems: long narrow plots behind the houses, dating from Medieval times.)

The county in general was becoming more wealthy at this time due to increased tin production. This expansion was followed by a rise in population and new enclosures of moor or common land for agriculture.

The ports of Cornwall also became more prosperous, and, with the increase in wealth, local gentry began building their manor houses with associated walled gardens. By the 15th century the upper classes could speak and write in English, (the rest of the population still conversed in their native Cornish); ideas from books and literature began to filter down and fashionable architectural styles became more widespread.

Deer parks also became popular again and many manor houses, large and small, had their deer, mainly as a status symbol.

Although, in British terms, Cornwall became relatively prosperous and had access to the fashionable conceits of the day, the Venetian ambassador to Castille, who was held up by bad weather at Falmouth in 1506, was less than impressed and wrote in disparaging terms: "We are in a very wild

place which no human being ever visits, in the midst of a barbarous race, so different in language and custom from the Londoners and the rest of England that they are as unintelligible to the last as to Venetians"!

By the time of the dissolution of the monasteries in 1536 there were many wealthy enough to benefit and buy the monastic lands. At the end of the century Carew referred to this as "the golden shower of the dissolved abbey lands [that] rained well near into every gaper's mouth". Out of their plunder, the gentry of Cornwall built new houses, enlarged old ones and by 1540 when John Leland visited, he was able to see "pretty woods and fair grounds" surrounding the manor houses. Gardens became increasingly important and the garden was also brought indoors by means of colourful and complicated tapestries showing cherubs disporting themselves in formal gardens and amongst foliage, such as can still be seen in the 'verdure' hangings at Cotehele. The accompanying illustration of the beautiful hanging in the Punch room at Cotehele clearly shows a complicated parterre garden with a large variety of clipped trees in the background.

Cotehele: the Verdure Tapestries in the Punch Room

Although the mid-16th century was often a troubled time rife with wars, religious discord and privateering, the strategic importance of the Far West in war and as a springboard to the New World became increasingly relevant, with many rich and influential families having Cornish connections and property.

It is at this time that the first depiction of a Cornish garden is to be found – on Lord Burghley's chart of Falmouth harbour, drawn in the late 16th century. This shows the manor house of Arwennack (the home of the swashbuckling and piratical Killigrews) as having a typical 16th-century garden with a number of walled enclosures, one featuring a maze.

It was also at this time that Mount Edgcumbe house was built to a revolutionary design, framed by an avenue of trees leading down to the water's edge – an unusual feature at a time when most gardens were enclosed and inward-looking.

By the beginning of the 17th century the tin industry was also becoming more prosperous, due to the old-fashioned method of tin streaming being replaced by mining. Families such as the Godolphins were made fabulously rich by their mining activities, and used their wealth not only for new buildings but also to construct a complicated garden with raised walks, fishponds and knot gardens. Today, these features are being uncovered and indicate that Cornwall was certainly no backwater in matters of fashion and garden design.

The view from Hall Walk, Fowey, in 1904

The late 16th century chart of Falmouth Haven in Lord Burghley's collection showing Arwennack just below the castle

Walks were also a fashionable feature throughout the county, one particularly famous example being at Hall Walk, Fowey, where flowers and summerhouses lined the path overlooking the beautiful (and at that time strategically significant) Fowey River.

The build-up to the Civil War and the war itself was to change prosperity to disaster, even after the Restoration of the monarchy in 1660 life was still difficult for some time. Gradually, however, things began to improve and the rise of merchants, lawyers and tin barons led to widespread re-building and associated garden-making.

(above) **Edmund Prideaux's drawing of Stowe in its heyday (circa 1720) and** *(below)* **the earth banks at Stowe today**

The simple enclosed garden at Truthan – from a map by George Withiel in 1690

The small enclosed gardens of the 16th and early 17th centuries gave way to much more elaborate creations with Italianate features. Although many smaller gardens were still simple and enclosed, the view out of the garden became more important and terraced gardens with statues and balustrades in imitation of the Italian villa began to be constructed. These can be seen in the exotically titled "Black Book of Spoure", a well illustrated manuscript dating from 1690 which contains sketches of all the properties belonging to the family. Penheale is shown with a fine set of steps, and other gardens in the county have terraced features and formal planting. In contrast to these relatively simple gardens belonging to the lesser gentry was the manor at Stowe (in north Cornwall) which was constructed in 1679 for John Grenville, first Earl of Bath, and by 1694 was surrounded by extensive formal gardens containing a series of walled spaces with fruit trees, pavilions and elaborate parterres.

In 1701, little more than 20 years after he had built Stowe, John Grenville died, and although his son and grandson succeeded, both were dead by 1711. The house was uninhabited, and ultimately in 1739, demolished. All that remains today are a few walls and extensive earthworks, which can now only be easily interpreted from aerial photographs.

The Eighteenth Century

Other great houses, however, did not meet such a fate – the 18th-century capitalist society resulted in great fortunes being made, particularly from mining.

William Lemon, for example, the son of a poor man from Germoe, became immensely rich and bought the estate at Carclew near Truro. He

Mount Edgcumbe – Badeslade's illustration of 1735

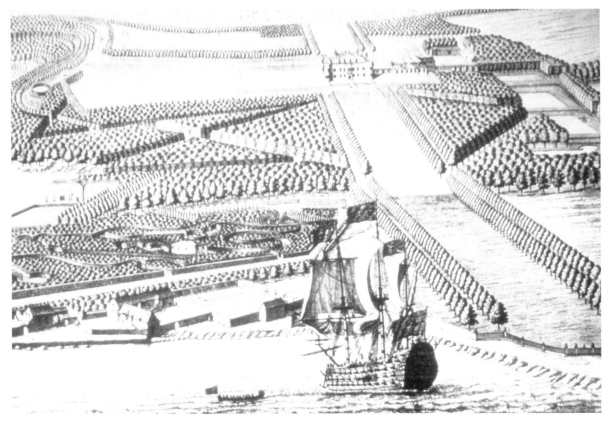

The 18th century Bath House at Penrose

finished the house and from 1745 onwards laid out extensive gardens with serpentine paths, walled and water gardens, plantations and a deer park. These serpentine paths in the style advocated by Stephen Switzer were becoming old fashioned by this time, so perhaps they were laid out according to the designs intended by his predecessor.

The earliest enclosed formal gardens such as Prideaux gave way to grand schemes like Mount Edgcumbe, which became increasingly complicated with a highly structured landscape containing ruins,

follies, shrubberies and extensive plantings. Large hedges were a particular feature of the mid-18th century, clipped to form allées and enclosing wildernesses, all of which can be seen in Badeslade's illustration of Mount Edgcumbe dating from 1735.

From the mid-18th century onwards, classical influences bacame predominant; many wealthy landowners had carried out "the Grand Tour" of Italy, visiting all the well known classical sites, and were also heavily influenced by the landscape paintings of Claude Lorraine and Salvator Rosa.

Classical antiquities such as triumphal arches (as at Werrington), rustic hermitages, bath houses and cascades (at Tehidy) were introduced into the wider landscapes surrounding the house, where they were not just viewed as attractive objects but as inspiration to arouse thought of aesthetic principles, and even in some cases as a source of political satire.

The Mid-late 18th Century – Opening Up the Landscape

A reaction against these 'constructed' landscapes took place from the middle of the century onwards with the influence of Capability Brown. Brown, although he never visited Cornwall, was highly

The Triumphal Arch at Werrington

An early 19th century view of Trelissick

influential in the move towards opening up the view and leaving the house "grazing" in the landscape by demolishing all the more formal features that had surrounded it.

Brown's influence was still around right up until the end of the 18th century, when a certain Mr Gray in laying out the landscapes at Heligan,

Prideaux and Menabilly caused Mr Rashleigh (of Prideaux, near St Austell) to remark that Gray was "a strict and bigoted pupil of the modern school – that which the famous Capability Brown founded... he was all for shaving the lawn and dotting it with clumps and confining it with a belt; and is entirely ignorant or insensible to the beauty which now is recognised in so many of the old places where the House is surrounded by an ornamental garden, flower parterres, terraces and balustrades, all calculated to give ideas of comfort and to present to the eye and taste a thousand beautiful and contrasted objects. He had been employed at Menabilly and in destroying the formal features... entirely divested it of its charm... it is now nothing more than a house in a tame, flat field." (Ref: Memoirs of Sir Colman Rashleigh. F.S. 3/1127/1/2.)

Humphry Repton

The next influential figure to be involved in Cornish gardens was Humphry Repton. It is surprising, in view of the dreadful reputation of Cornish roads, that he ever managed to set foot in the county; but he did manage to visit on a few occasions, very possibly at the insistence of the then Prime Minister, Pitt the Younger, who had extensive estates at Boconnoc. Repton was first to give an opinion on Mount Edgcumbe, which was already one of the most fashionable places to visit and where he was only to titivate around the edges on

Repton's proposals for Trewarthenick – before (above) **and after** (below)

Caerhays – a north-east view in the 19th century

behalf of Pitt's sister who was married to the Earl.

Also in the east of the county he produced Red Books (with his famous before and after pictures) for Port Eliot (1792), Catchfrench (1792), Pentillie (1809) and possibly Coldrenick. During his second visit in 1809, the furthest west he was to travel was Tregothnan (1809) where the new Gothic mansion was being built — the landscape today, with wonderful views of the river framed by woodland, is thought to be a result of Repton's involvement. He produced a Red Book for nearby Trewarthenick in 1793 (which can be seen at the County Record Office), suggesting typical tree belts and a lake (although these plans were not acted upon until some years later). Indeed, Sarah Gregor, the owner's daughter, was somewhat scathing in her diaries regarding the proximity of pigsties, which were later to be removed as part of Repton's proposals.

Finally, it is also possible that the new Nash edifice at Caerhays Castle owed some of its landscape setting to the involvement of Repton, although his hitherto amicable partnership with Nash had come to an end by 1809.

In contrast to all the grandiose schemes of the wealthy landowners were the small plots of the miners and agricultural labourers, which had remained unchanged for hundreds of years. C S Gilbert in 1820 referred to many of the cottagers having "a garden containing esculent roots and vegetables, an apple tree or two with gooseberry and currant bushes. Cultivation of leeks, onions and parsley took place – articles essential in the formation of pies." The Cornish have always been well known for their passion for pies (or pasties), having made pies of almost everything eatable – herby pies, potato pie, squab pie, maggoty (magpie?) pie and pilchard pie; indeed, it is said that the Devil would never cross the Tamar for fear of being put into a pie!

Potatoes in particular were grown enthusiastically, the majority of miners setting out potato plots as part of their clearance of the moorland and its subsequent conversion into thousands of tiny walled fields.

The 19th Century

As the 19th century progressed, gardens became even more complicated and overflowing with plants – the latter mainly as a result of the vast influx of specimens from plant hunters who were scouring the world for exotics suitable for growing at home.

The Lobb Brothers – Plant Hunters Extraordinaire

Two of the most successful Victorian plant hunters were the brothers William and Thomas Lobb. Although born at Pencarrow in 1809 and 1817 respectively, they spent their formative years at Carclew, where that formidable plantsman Sir Charles Lemon encouraged them and nurtured their horticultural aspirations. It was through his recommendations that both brothers were to be employed by the famous nursery firm, Vietch's of Exeter.

William was the first to leave Britain, sailing for Buenos Aires in 1840. He travelled across the Andes where he collected seed of the Monkey Puzzle, *Araucaria araucana*, (named after the Araucarian Indians). Although collected by Menzies in 1795 and James McRae in 1824, Lobb's consignment was the first substantial importation, enabling widespread distribution of seedlings. Indeed, it was at Pencarrow that the name Monkey Puzzle was coined (see Gazetteer entry).

William also collected many other fine plants including *Desfontainea spinosa*, *Embothrium coccineum* and the lovely climber, *Lapageria rosea*. His South American conifers included *Podocarpus nubigenus* and *Saxegothaea conspicua* (the latter can still be seen at Scorrier House, grown from original seed).

Following his South American expeditions, William set out for California in 1849. Here in the mountains of Oregon and the Sierra Nevada he found *Thuya plicata* (now *T. lobbii*), *Abies grandis* and *Torreya californica*, and the impressive *Sequoiadendron giganteum* or *Wellingtonia*. (It has been said that Lobb insisted it be named Wellingtonia after the Mount Wellington mine near his home in Cornwall.)

Lobb continued to introduce many other species of note, including *Abutilon vitifolium* and *Lomatia ferruginea*, which grow particularly successfully in Cornish gardens, sheltered by his useful South American introduction, *Escallonia macrantha*.

William died in California in 1863; his brother Thomas, in contrast, was to return to his native Devoran to end his days quietly, after spending 17 years travelling in the Far East and Indian sub-continent.

Like William, he was sent out by Veitch's, initially to Java in 1843. Stopping off in Singapore, he made his first collections, mainly pitcher plants and tropical rhododendrons.

Travelling on to Java, he discovered a rich hunting ground, particularly for orchids including *Vanda tricolor*, *Bulbophyllum lobbii* and a host of others.

After a short trip home he set out again, arriving in Calcutta in 1849 on his way to Sarawak and the Philippines. Returning via Burma he discovered the beautiful scented rhododendron, *R. veitchianum*. Thence to India, where he was to collect 'one man's load' of the desirable blue orchid *Vanda coerulea*. The famous plant hunter Joseph Dalton Hooker was also in India at that time. Although the two men met briefly in the Khasia Hills they apparently did not have much to say to each other. Hooker recorded his meeting with Lobb whom he found to be "a most steady and respectable man and modest and well behaved in his deportment, but dreadfully conceited"! He also noted that Lobb pooh-poohed Sikkim and had a very poor opinion of Lindley and Wallis, the two collectors.

In spite of Lobb's opinion, the borders of Nepal were rich in treasures. Thomas was to discover the impressive *Cardiocrinum giganteum*, which was amply to satisfy the competitive instincts of English gardeners who would vie with each other to grow the tallest specimens - it has been known to reach an amazing 12 feet (3.7m)!

In the summer of 1854 Thomas again visited Java where he acquired several Japanese plants from the Dutch East India Company garden at Buitenzorg. Included was *Cryptomeria japonica* var. *lobbii* and *C. japonica elegans*; specimens of both can be seen in a number of Cornish gardens, with a particularly impressive specimen of the former at Boconnoc.

Thomas was buried in Devoran churchyard, where a number of shrubs that he introduced were planted by Bishop Hunkin in the 1930s. Recently, plans have been put forward to develop a Lobb garden at Baldhu church, under the auspices of the Tregellas Foundation.

Today, when we look around us at the thousands of plants from all corners of the world that flourish in our gardens, we must not forget the intrepid travels of two unassuming Cornish men who roamed the world and of whom Edward Hyams would later remark, "not even Hooker did more for the environment of the European and American flora".

List of Australian Seeds for Cornwall.

Acacia decurrens.	Black Wattle.	tree.	30 to 100 feet.
" diffusa.	The spreading Acacia.	shrub	3 to 5 ft.
" melanoxylon.	Blackwood or Lightwood.	tree.	40 to 150 ft.
Bellendenia montana.	Mountain Bellendenia.	shrub.	1 ft.
Billardiera longiflora.	Long-flowered Apple Berry.	twiner.	
Bursaria spinosa.	Prickly Native Box.	tree.	10 to 20 feet.
Casuarina distyla.	Stunted She-oak.	shrub.	10 ft
" quadrivalvis.	Coast or Drooping she-oak.	tree.	30 to 50 ft.
" suberosa.	Erect She-oak.	tree.	30 to 40 ft.
Cyathodes acerosa.	Needle-leaved Cyathodes.	shrub.	3 ft.
Dianella tasmanica.	Broad-leaved Native Flax Lily.	perennial.	
Drimys axillaris.	New Zealand Pepper Tree.	tree.	10 to 30 ft.
Drymophila cyanocarpa.	Blue-berried Drymophila.	perennial.	
Eucalyptus alpina.	Alpine Gum.	small tree.	10 to 15 ft.
" coccifera.	Kermes Gum.	tree.	30 ft.
" cordata.	Heart-shaped-leaved Gum.	tree.	50 ft.
Goodia latifolia.	Salisbury Pea.	shrub.	4 to 8 ft.
Hakea eriantha.	Woolly-flowered Hakea.	tree.	8 to 15 ft.
Indigofera australis.	Australian Indigo Plant.	shrub	2 to 6
Metrosideros tomentosa.	New Zealand Fire Tree.	tree.	40 to 50 ft
Prostanthera lasianthos.	Victorian Dogwood or Mint Tree.	tree.	20 to 30 ft
Richea dracophylla.	Dragon-leaf Richea.	shrub or small tree.	5 to 12 ft.

Correspondence with Australia *(above and overleaf)* **to G R Carlyon of Tregrehan during the age of plant hunting**

The crinkle-crankle wall at Killiow

Individuals such as Joseph Hooker introduced many rhododendrons from the hill ranges of India. Seeds were distributed amongst many of the Cornish gardens thus providing the basis for the many famous rhododendron gardens seen today.

The Cornish Lobb brothers *(see page 22)* were sent by Veitch (from the famous Exeter nursery) to the opposite ends of the world. William went to the Americas where he found many conifers and spectacular climbers, whilst Thomas visited Java and Indonesia searching for beautiful orchids for the hothouses of the day.

The expansion in the number and design of glasshouses was enormous, with particular impetus given by Sir Joseph Paxton of Crystal Palace fame. Greenhouses were built for pineapples, peaches, vines, melons, bananas and orchids; all with their different shapes, ventilation requirements and heating. Extensive experiments were carried out

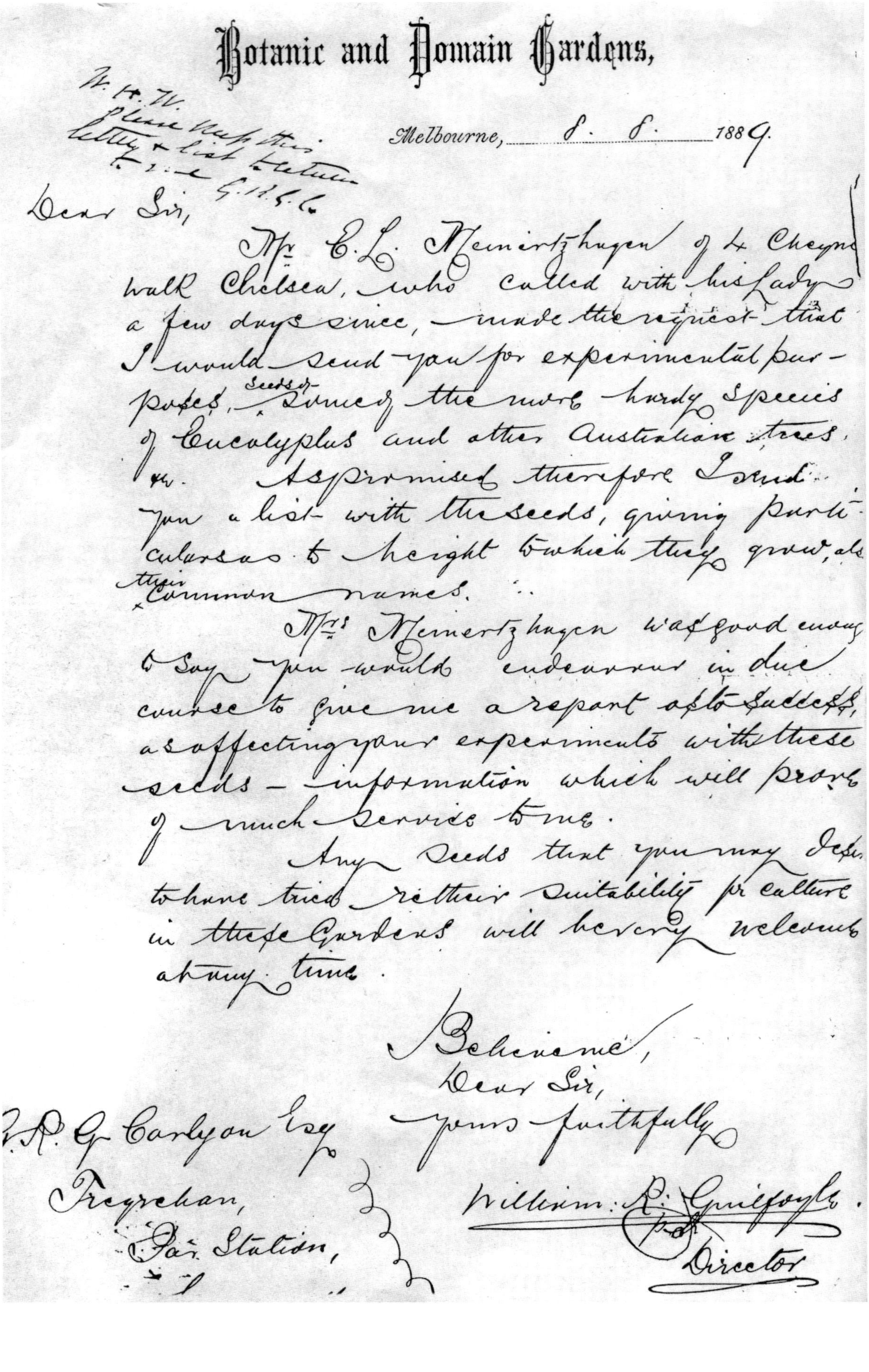

Botanic and Domain Gardens,

Melbourne, 8. 8. 1889.

W. & W.
Please keep this letter & list & return to me G.R.G.C.

Dear Sir,

Mr E. L. Meinertzhagen of 4 Cheyne walk Chelsea, who called with his Lady a few days since, made the request that I would send you for experimental purposes, seeds of some of the more hardy species of Eucalyptus and other Australian trees &c. As promised therefore I send you a list with the seeds, giving particulars as to height to which they grow, also their common names.

Mrs Meinertzhagen was good enough to say you would endeavour in due course to give me a report as to success, as affecting your experiments with these seeds – information which will prove of much service to me.

Any seeds that you may desire to have tried re their suitability for culture in these Gardens will be very welcome at any time.

Believe me,
Dear Sir,
Yours faithfully
William R. Guilfoyle.
per
Director

T. R. G. Carlyon Esq.
Tregrehan,
Par Station,

(above) **The greenhouse at Prideaux in the 19th century**
(below) **An aerial view of the Nesfield Terrace at Tregrehan c. 1938**

**The Downes, Hayle, from J D Sedding's
Garden Craft Old and New 1891**

and the gardening magazines of the day were full of correspondence.

In Cornwall such places as Heligan, Tregrehan and Porthgwidden were particularly famous for their glasshouses; competitive spirit raged, the owners vying for the prize for the largest and heaviest pineapple or the most unusual fruit. Complicated structures such as walled gardens with "crinkle crankle" walls (to capture the heat more effectively) were built as at Killiow, and the slanting beds at Trengwainton were also built at this time.

In design terms, as the Victorian age progressed, anything and everything was tried. Vast rockeries were constructed, as at Pencarrow. American gardens, Japanese gardens, exotic gardens and Italian gardens all were the height of fashion at some point in the 19th century. The Italian garden was a particular speciality of William Nesfield, who produced many designs involving 'parterres de broderie' (elaborate patterns outlined in box enhanced by coloured earths and gravels), terraces, balustrades and classical statues.

Nesfield's only known involvement in Cornwall was at Tregrehan, where his design was for a terrace in front of the house with parterres, sundial and pool. This lay-out survived until the 1970s and can be clearly be seen on an early aerial photograph of the house.

Towards the end of the century, however, a reaction set in against the complexities and extravagances of the early Victorian period, and the 'wild gardening principles' of William Robinson became influential. Instead of structured and formal areas, shrubberies with swathes of under-planted wild flowers became more fashionable and it is largely on these principles that many of the existing gardens of Cornwall have been laid out.

In contrast to the Robinsonian tradition, John Dando Sedding, who wrote "Garden-Craft Old and New" in 1890, aimed for a more formal lay-out based on the earlier Tudor gardens, with clipped yews, symmetrical paths and beds nearer to the house, which were to lead gradually into the wild areas at the edge of the garden.

The only known Sedding garden has recently been rediscovered at The Downes, Hayle (not open to the public) and although little now exists of the former planting, the basic structure of the lay-out as described in The British Architect of 1887 is still apparent.

The 20th Century

Sedding's formality was echoed by Sir Edwin Lutyens and Gertrude Jekyll at Penheale in the period following the First World War. The latter half of the 19th century also saw the rapid expansion of the tourist industry, with the Great Western Railway promoting the Cornish Riviera. Visitors began to arrive in their thousands, and public parks such as those in Penzance and Falmouth were laid out specifically for the enjoyment of the holidaymakers.

Public parks were also to be made for the local inhabitants in all the larger towns, and there are a number of "Victoria Gardens" named after the Queen. Some of these public parks were constructed from designs drawn up by landscape architects such as Reginald Upcher at Penzance and F.W. Meyer at Truro whilst others incorporated existing large gardens or estates which were either willed to or bought by the council. The latter included the Fox Rosehill and Gyllyngdune gardens in Falmouth and Thankes Park at Torpoint.

The heyday of the public park was in late Victorian and Edwardian times, but the advent of the First World War was to bring about many changes both to the public and private garden.

The war brought to an end many of the Victorian gardens – life had changed radically and there were too few men returning from the conflict to re-create the splendours they had left behind. Gardens which had thirty-five gardeners before 1914 now had to make do with a mere handful, and many gardens grew neglected and their greenhouses lay unused.

An early postcard of Penzance showing Morrab Gardens

Restoration at Heligan – the Italian Garden before *(above)* **and after** *(below)*

Reginald Upcher's design for Morrab Gardens, Penzance of 1888

The Second World War seemed to be the final death knell for the Grand Gardens – few retained their splendours and many trees and shrubs were lost as a result of weather and time.

Today the tide of gardening has changed to that of the smaller garden, created very often by "retired" folk. Many of these gardens are based on a generally informal lay-out but some, more recently, have a more formally designed basis, such as at Bosvigo, Truro.

The larger gardens still exist, however, and restorations such as those at Mount Edgcumbe and Heligan have not only rescued the dying gardens but have injected new vigour. Restorations, as well as renewing the planting and lay-outs, can show technology and working conditions as well as the plants that were important at the time the gardens were first laid out.

All of our gardens are a dynamic entity, never standing still; they continue to evolve, some disappearing completely, some re-emerging, and others born of new ideas.

In conclusion, Katherine Lee Jenner's poem seems particularly apt:

> "While here on every hand
> Is still the record of our fathers' lives,
> Though their hopes and fears
> Have passed away like sunlight on the hills
> Down through the path of years."

from "Old Names" by Katherine Lee Jenner
(For full poem see "Cornish Chorus"
edited by M. Hawkey, 1948.)

Sue Pring

Plants and Planting

Wildings and Exotics

Cornwall, although a relatively treeless county (having a tree cover of only 3% as far back in time as the Domesday survey) nevertheless has a wide variety of different habitats.

The deep sheltered valleys still contain oak woodlands, formerly coppices which were used to provide both charcoal for tin smelting and bark for tanning. In contrast are the open moorlands and the hedgerows of the cultivated lands. Although the far west (Penwith) has many stone walls and the east of the county has earth banks, the majority of Cornish hedges are unlike those of the rest of the country in that they are a solid construction of two parallel walls of stone infilled with earth, with a living hedge planted on the top. Until the advent of Dutch Elm disease, the majority of hedges had many elms (Ulmus species) growing out of them — not just for shelter but also (in historic times) to be used as timber. Once cut down, they would very usefully renew themselves from the stump. Many of the tiny Cornish lanes are thought to have been in existence for thousands of years, the deep, tree-covered tunnels helping to shelter both the traveller and the associated plants.

Celia Fiennes, that indefatigable traveller of the late 17th century, wrote in her book ("Through England on a Side Saddle") of riding "as if in a grove in most places, regular rows of trees standing on each side of the road". Later, however, in the early 18th century, Tonkin disagreed with the habit of leaving the trees to grow, complaining that he had received "irreparable injury from riding beneath overhanging branches".

A coastal stone hedge with foxgloves and thrift near The Rumps

Carpobrotus edulis **on the Lizard**

Although the landscape has changed radically both visually and ecologically owing to the death of the elms over the last decade, the hedges themselves still retain a wide variety of herbaceous flora, unlike those of many other counties.

The springtime brings the pink, white and blue of campions, stitchwort and bluebells; followed in the summer by foxgloves and gorse. Cowslips flourish on hedgerows close to the sea, where blown sand creates a more alkaline soil. Also near the sea are edible plants such as sea beet, Alexanders and the rare Babington's Leek (the latter two plants being ancient naturalized cultivars).

The more shady hedgerows have wonderful colonies of ferns, particularly the Hart's Tongue, together with primroses, mosses and lichens. Primroses are abundant and have been since ancient times, the Celtic month of April (Mis Ebrall) being named after the plant. Valley bottoms often contain the remnants of former willow gardens where two varieties of willow were grown, to be used for basketry and cooperage and, particularly in a maritime country, for crab pots and fish traps.

The moorlands and heathlands have a completely different flora — one particularly special area on the Lizard peninsula is said to be second only to Teesdale for botanical riches. Many rare plants are to be found here, the best known being the Cornish Heath (Erica vagans), discovered by Ray in 1667. Its showy densely packed flower heads have formed the basis for many horticultural cultivars including the famous 'Lyonesse', a white variety, and 'St Keverne' which has rose pink flowers. Before becoming appreciated by gardeners, the heather (or 'griglan') was used in a practical fashion to make brushes and brooms.

Another feature of the heathlands and hedge banks is common gorse (*Ulex europaeus*) together with another lower-growing type, the Western gorse (*Ulex gallii*). The ubiquitous nature of gorse or furze throughout the county is almost certainly due to its former importance as a fuel. In a treeless county, it was particularly useful for heating the Cornish clay (or clome) bread ovens. It was also used for fodder, both as tender young shoots and also after having been crushed through a type of mill; and even as a manure for apple trees.

As well as the carpets of native flowers on the hedges and headlands, a number of cultivated plants can be found growing as "escapes" throughout the county. The red, pink and sometimes white valerian (*Centranthus ruber*) grows out of walls in the vicinity of settlements, as does the Mexican daisy (*Erigeron karvinskianus* syn. *E. mucronatus*).

More of a threat to the native flora is the Hottentot Fig (*Carpobrotus edulis*) a mat-forming succulent with large daisy-like flowers of bright purple, pink or yellow. In some areas, notably the Lizard, the existing carpets of thrift, sea campion and kidney vetch are being smothered by this invader which although very attractive has proved difficult to eradicate where it is not required.

The Isles of Scilly have even more exotic escapes including aeonium species, agapanthus and ixias. The mild conditions which enable these exotics to flourish in the wilder areas outside the garden are also ideal for the cultivation of many rare and tender plants within the confines of the garden wall.

Borlase's illustration of an aloe, 1757

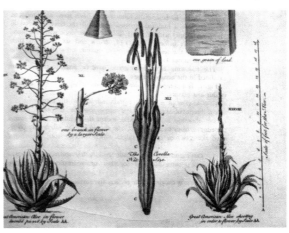

Exotics at Lamorran garden, St Mawes

Clianthus puniceus (Parrot's Bill)

such as the Canary palm (*Chamaerops canariensis*) at Trewidden. Most amazing of all are the Tree Ferns, many of which are almost a hundred years old and have reached prodigious sizes in gardens such as Trebah, Heligan and Bosahan; and, of course, in the remarkable fern pit at Trewidden.

It is not only the private gardens that contain these tender treasures. The public gardens at Penzance have a good range of exotic specimens. Morrab Gardens has a collection of colletias including the incredible anchor plant, *Colletia cruciata*, and the scented *Colletia armata* where the approaching bees and butterflies have to negotiate formidable spines before collecting the nectar.

Falmouth has Fox-Rosehill Gardens where tender species have been grown for over a hundred years; whilst more recently a collection of palms has been created with bananas, aloes and other succulents adding to the tropical atmosphere.

As F H Hamilton Davey so aptly said in 1897: "the climate of Cornwall has successfully wooed into obedience floral varieties from the temperate to equatorial zones... No longer have we to go to our stove-houses to see the lordly Banana, the stately Furcrea, the musk scented Olearia, the Citron and the Orange. We have them all growing in the open, where, summer and winter alike, we may behold them clothed in all their beauty".

National Plant Collections in Cornwall

Further information from NCCPG Directory:

Acacia – Tresco Abbey Gardens
Bambuseae (Phyllostachys var.) – (private garden)
Camellia – Mount Edgcumbe
Canna – Brockings Nursery, N. Petherwin
Coleus – Brockings Nursery, N. Petherwin
Crocosmia – Lanhydrock
Dahlia – Rosewarne
Grevillea – Pine Lodge Gardens, St Austell
Hemerocallis – Antony House
Malus (Cornish apple var.) – Trelissick (not a National Collection)
Nothofagus – Tavistock Woodland Estate, Gunnislake
Viola odorata – private garden
Viola – a collection of old varieties can be seen at Heligan

Sue Pring

The majority of Cornish gardens, particularly in the west of the county, contain plants that are particularly tender. Gardeners have always been prone to attempting the impossible and the Cornish are no exception — many plants which in theory cannot be grown in Britain flourish outside, perhaps to be annihilated once every few years by a particularly bad winter, but often surviving in spite of snow, storm and tempest. As early as 1757, Borlase described and illustrated the flowering of his precious aloe.

Today, Tresco on the Isles of Scilly is, of course, the pièce de la résistance of tender gardens, but many other gardens have 'exotics'. Lamorran, near St Mawes, has recently been planted with a fine collection of Mediterranean plants such as cycads and palms, with acacias, cacti and eucalypts adding to the effect. St Michael's Mount and Headland Garden also have many tender rockery plants that flourish in spite of being regularly blasted by the sea.

Older gardens, mostly dating from the Victorian period, contain ancient specimens of tender species

The History of Bamboos in Cornwall

Although the first bamboo to be planted in England in 1827 was *Phyllostachys nigra*, the Black Bamboo, it was not until the end of the 19th century that bamboo fever gripped explorers and large quantities of new species were imported. All were considered exotic and the sheltered gardens of Cornwall were the first to receive these treasures of unknown hardiness. Some were imported from hotter areas and subsequently found to be completely hardy, others, from areas like China and Japan with generally hotter summers but colder winters, were also found to be mainly hardy (although often less vigorous). Plants from the higher reaches of the Himalayas were invariably found to be very hardy, graduating to plants from lower elevations which were only suited to Cornish or west coast gardens with their cool humid weather.

As plants are mainly classified by their flowers, and bamboos rarely flower, these plants were introduced under various names; some native names, some incorrect and some according with current classification. This was further complicated by different native regional names for the same species and some native names covering different species of similar habit. Most great Cornish gardens have accurate records of species received and their progress.

The general conclusion for Cornish gardens is that during the period 1890 to 1900 several large batches of bamboo imports were received each year but when all the synonyms are eliminated these reduce down to about 30 different species and cultivars.

Most species quickly found the cool humid conditions in the South West very much to their liking and old photographs from before the turn of the century are available in some estates showing proud owners standing next to huge plants. Unfortunately for the future cultivation of bamboos, the only species distributed from Cornwall to the colder regions of Britain were mainly the few rampant species that the owners must have been glad to dispose of (*Sasa palmata*, *Pseudosasa japonica*, etc.) So bamboos are labelled to this day in Britain as being either very tender or extremely rampant which is far from the truth. The beautiful and well behaved species such as *Fargesia nitida* and *Fargesia murielea* and many others are much prized over the rest of mainland Europe.

Bamboo at Morrab Gardens c. 1895

Drepanostachyum hookerianum at Fox Rosehill Gardens

Much has been said of the flamboyant mood in all avenues of life after the turn of the century, and this seems to have been reflected in our gardens as well. Enthusiasm for plant form changed overnight into apathy and all records early this century concentrated on impressive flowering plants. This was the start of the period of decline of bamboos in Cornwall. Ten years ago, just before the renewed interest in them, probably two thirds of the plants had vanished from Cornish gardens. It is hard to understand how robust plants often over 8m (26ft) high can disappear completely. One plant of *Phyllostachys viridis* 'Robert Young' 11.50m (38ft) high was recorded by Bean at Trebah in 1942 but there was no sign of it 30 years later.

These plants have always had a high value; because of the rarity and slow root growth of the more desirable species, it is possible some were sold as family fortunes fluctuated. Others were weakened by the heavy shade of the maturing trees. Although this in itself would not normally kill a bamboo, in combination with the rare event of flowering, which seriously weakens even a robust specimen, the plant would be doomed. Some bamboos (such as *Drepanostachyum falcatum* and *D. falconeri*) never recover after flowering, but set ample seed; this has happened during the last few years with the above species at Bosloe, Penjerrick and Fox Rosehill.

Due to changes in fashion, more recent introductions such as the beautiful South American bamboo *Chusquea culeou* are rare in the county, though this species has recently been planted at Carwinion near Falmouth. Fortunately parallel with the interest in the restoration of old gardens, desire has developed in a few gardens to restore these beautiful plants to their former eminence.

Fine collections can be seen in Cornwall at Carwinion and Trebah, where many good new introductions as well as the traditional species can be seen. Another garden where the surviving species have been restored is Heligan, which contains a wide selection of early introductions. As far as is known the largest *Phyllostachys edulis* and *Phyllostachys bambusoïdes* in this country are to be found at Penjerrick, the largest *Chimonobambusa quadrangularis* at Heligan.

As it only happens at long intervals, the flowering of bamboos is a very important event for botanists. Some species have never been recorded in flower and so cannot be accurately classified. Cornwall has had two such important events in the last few years. *Fargesia nitida* recently flowered for the first recorded time at Carwinion, the first since its importation by seed in 1889. An even rarer event was the discovery of only two flowers on *Chimonobambusa quadrangularis* at Heligan. These are the only flowers ever recorded in the world on this species; there is not even any record of flowering in its native China or in Japan where it is naturalised.

Just west of Lanivet are the remains of the plantations and drying sheds of the Bamboo Cane Company, the only commercial venture in the UK producing home-grown canes. This was begun during the Second World War to replace imported canes and operated for about 30 years. Good quality canes were produced, but the high cost of labour to cut, remove branches and clean the culms made the business uncompetitive in times of peace. Roadworks together with the recent extensive flowering of the two main species have decimated the plantations, but the hill behind St Bennetts is still an enchanting place for the bamboo enthusiast.

England is one of the most favourable places in the world for growing temperate bamboos and Cornwall, therefore, holds a unique place for bamboo cultivation. There is nowhere else in this country where bamboos can be seen growing on almost every estate. The cool humid conditions allow us to grow the elongated mountain species which dislike hot summers as successfully as both the temperate low level species and those that cannot endure cold winters. Visitors from all over the world come to see these little-understood plants, including scientists from the Orient anxious to see and learn about their native species growing to maturity in a different environment.

Mike Bell

Magnolias, Rhododendrons and Camellias

An introduction to the stalwarts of the Cornish Spring garden

It was not in my father's nature to be jealous; however, there used to be a touch of envy in his voice when he talked of the gardens that hugged the south coast of Cornwall as being in the "Banana Country"! There is no doubt that these southern gardens, Trengwainton and such like, are a degree of two warmer than my own garden at Chyverton in the winter, but all Cornish gardens grow an immense range of exotic flora, benefiting from the effect of the Gulf Stream – its effect dramatically illustrated by comparing lowest winter temperatures of Cornwall -7°C (20°F) with those of Newfoundland on the same degree of latitude -23°C (-10°F).

Temperature is not the only climatic factor that controls what is grown in Cornish gardens; rainfall of 40 to 60 inches (102-153cm) is a help, but the key factor (a major disadvantage) is wind. Severe gales are commonplace and many plants will not grow happily in Cornwall without shelter. It is the wind which has led to the creation of the typical "Cornish garden", a collection of plants growing in a sheltered valley with good tree cover. Classic examples are found bordering the Helford River, Bosahan, Glendurgan and Trebah. Nearby is Penjerrick: created early in the 19th century by a member of the Fox family, this is my role-model –

a bosky valley running south, protected by fine trees sheltering exotic shrubs originating from all the continents of the world, with a carpet of wild flowers and ferns growing in that essential for a Cornish garden – an acid soil.

Less typical are the gardens that have been created within great estates, with landscaping around the mansion house, dating from the 18th century or earlier, such as Boconnoc, Lanhydrock, Mount Edgcumbe, Port Eliot and Tregothnan.

Although many of these great estates originally had their deer parks and plantations, much of the rest of the county had been subject to the demands of mining and tin smelting which led to destruction or coppicing... "[In 1656] 20,000 cartloads of wood, worth £375, were coled (made into charcoal) on the spot, and carried to the Melting Houses from Lantyan Wood on the River Fowey." (Thurston).

As early as 1800 this loss of woodland due to mining was recognised by John Thomas of Chyverton, a Vice Warden of the Stannaries. He summoned the landowners of Cornwall to a meeting in Truro; there was a splendid response. Calling themselves The Men of The Trees, they

Woodland carpeted with wild flowers at Trehane

Stems of the ancient *Magnolia grandiflora* at Lanhydrock

resolved to plant trees. John Thomas set a good example – whereas in 1770 there was only a small copse protecting his house from the prevailing westerlies, by the time of his death in 1825 there were 94 acres of woodland. Without this legacy the garden at Chyverton would not exist; the same could be said of many other of the county's gardens. These early 19th century plantings give that essential protection required for the growing of tender and exotic trees and shrubs.

The meeting of The Men of The Trees could not have come at a more opportune time. Although the influx of plants into the British Isles began ten thousand years ago with the ending of the Ice Age, it was really not until the 19th century that there was a massive increase in the flow of plants into the British Isles due to the opening of borders between countries, better communication and the employment of the professional plant collector for the first time.

That is not to say, however, that in the intervening years no plants had reached these shores. The colonisation of the east coast of North America was of particular importance – the first magnolia came from Virginia in 1688. It had been collected by a curate sent out by Henry Compton, Bishop of London. A passionate lover of the exotic, the Bishop took advantage of the American colonies being part of the See of London – there was only one posting for any of his priests who showed botanical leanings! The Bishop built up a fabulous collection of exotics at Fulham Palace – unfortunately this was destroyed on the orders of his successor, (whose main interest was his stomach) in order that the garden could be devoted to vegetables!

Magnolia virginiana was followed early in the 18th century by *Magnolia grandiflora*, one of North America's finest exports. It is now widely planted throughout the world and was particularly favoured

by the Victorians as a wall plant; it can be seen propping up many a Cornish house. The oldest specimen is at Antony, believed to have been planted in c.1750. In contrast to the openness of America, China and Japan were both closed to foreigners, and although the first Chinese magnolia was introduced in 1790, it was not until 1888 that *Magnolia stellata* was sent from Japan.

The first camellia, *Camellia japonica*, arrived in 1695 having been smuggled out of Japan and was initially thought of as tender, being treated as a stove plant; it did not escape into the open garden until the 19th century. Many of these 19th century plantings still survive today, notably at Scorrier, Tregrehan and Tregothnan.

Whilst the rich flora of China and Japan was to remain undiscovered until the latter years of the 19th century, the discoveries in North America continued apace due to the energy of plant collectors such as William Lobb and David Douglas.

India was also to prove a rich hunting ground. Joseph Hooker was to collect 43 species of rhododendron during his visit to the Himalayas, particularly Sikkim, between 1848 and 1850. *Rhododendron arboreum*, a magnificent tree-like species, had already been introduced about 1810 from the temperate Himalayas and was flourishing, forming the backbone of many Cornish gardens.

***Rhododendron macabeanum* at Trewithen**

Magnolia sargentiana robusta at Trewithen

Rhododendron arboreum at Heligan

Hooker introductions, and their associated hybrids such as 'Sir Charles Lemon', were to change the face of the rhododendron garden. *R. arboreum, campylocarpum, falconeri, griffithianum* and *niveum* had a quality lacking in the North American species introduced earlier. Kew had great success in raising Hooker's seeds, which were then distributed nationwide. On his return, Hooker actively promoted his rhododendrons, convinced that they would flourish in the British climate; indeed, Cornwall seemed to grow them particularly well, "better than in Sikkim"!

Hooker is known to have stayed with Sir Charles Lemon at Carclew and owing to the close relationships of many of the Cornish gentry (Sir Charles's son-in-law was John Tremayne of Heligan) other gardens also benefited, including Tremough, Tregothnan, Killiow, Menabilly and Scorrier. The Foxes at Penjerrick also cultivated these new Himalayans and the Head Gardener, Samuel Smith, proved to be one of the most successful hybridizers of all time. Using the blood red *R. arboreum*, the yellow *campylocarpum* and the white *griffithianum*, Smith produced some exceptional hybrids. The late Lord Aberconway, creator of the garden at Bodnant, considered R. 'Penjerrick' the finest rhododendron hybrid ever raised; what is even more remarkable is that Smith, who was Head Gardener for 46 years from 1889-1935, only made eleven crosses, every one a winner. His secret was commonsense, only using the best forms as parents.

Rhododendron arboreum

Smith was raising his hybrids at the end of the 19th and the beginning of the 20th century, an exciting period for the Cornish gardener. Hooker's rhododendrons were now reaching their maturity (an article in 1896 on rhododendrons from Sikkim at Heligan mentions *R. falconeri* with 258 flower-heads and *R. thomsonii* 25ft high) and the trickle of plants that had been arriving from Japan and China over the past two hundred years became a flood.

An influential collector at the time was Charles Maries, who went to Japan in 1877 collecting on behalf of Veitch of Coombe Wood. He had great success, sending back over 500 species including *Enkianthus campanulatus* and *Viburnum tomentosum* 'Mariesii'. Although he went on to China in 1878, he experienced great difficulties, with the consequence that, on returning home in 1879, he told Veitch's that there was nothing left in China worth collecting! Sadly, Veitch's seem to have believed him as they did not send out another collector to China for twenty years. This collector was Ernest Henry Wilson who was dispatched to China in 1899 specifically to collect seeds and plants of *Davidia*, one of the most remarkable trees in cultivation. It had been discovered near the Tibetan border in 1869 by Père Armand David, a French missionary. (The French missionaries made many remarkable finds; Delavay was particularly successful, sending back over 200,000 specimens, of which 1500 species were new to science.) Wilson was sent out as

a result of the suggestion by Augustin Henry who had been horrified by the wholesale destruction of the native flora due to the demands of agriculture. His search for the *Davidia* makes fascinating reading – eventually he discovered a grove of twenty trees, some with seed which was sent back to Veitch's from where it was distributed. Specimens from this first batch of seed can be seen at a number of gardens, including Heligan and Tregrehan. Wilson was a very successful collector, introducing over 60 species of rhododendron including *R. calophytum* and some splendid magnolias that are now the glories of Cornish gardens – *M. sargentiana robusta*, *M. wilsonii*, and most significantly *M. sprengeri diva*. The only specimen of the latter in cultivation, growing at Veitch's nursery, was nearly lost in 1914 when the nursery closed down. Fortunately the unique specimen of *diva* was purchased at the closing down sale by John Charles Williams (1861-1939) of Caerhays and Werrington.

"JC" Williams was a giant amongst his contemporaries, a truly great plantsman. He was one of the first to recognise the value of the floral riches of China, purchasing from Veitch's many of Wilson's early introductions, which flourished at Caerhays and Werrington. So great was their success that JC headed a syndicate that employed George Forrest, who was to spend many years collecting in China on behalf of JC and his friends. The introductions from these expeditions were to change the face of the Cornish Garden.

Forrest (1873-1932), a Scotsman, was immensely successful, sending home unbelievable quantities of seed; in 1913 he sent no less than 200 kilos (440 lbs) of seed from 600 species. Many of these were rhododendrons; Forrest made over 5,000 gatherings of rhododendron seed during his career. All his herbarium material went to the Botanic Garden at Edinburgh for evaluation, the influx of new species forcing Edinburgh to revise completely the classification of the genus. But perhaps the Forrest introduction that makes the most impact on the modern garden is not a rhododendron, but a camellia, *C. saluenensis*.

There is some doubt as to when *saluenensis* first flowered at Caerhays, or when JC crossed it with *C. japonica*, thereby creating a new race of camellias. Given the collective epithet *williamsii*, there is hardly a garden in the world with suitable soil for camellias that does not grow one of the many varieties from *williamsii* parentage.

Other garden owners to benefit immediately from Forrest were JC's cousin P D Williams (Lanarth), E J P Magor (Lamellan) and G H Johnstone (Trewithen). Lanarth is remembered for a remarkable magnolia, *M. mollicomata* 'Lanarth', with deep fuschia-purple flowers. The plant has a

Tree ferns (*Dicksonia antartica*) at Trebah

particular significance to me – a seedling given to my father in 1954 by P D Williams' son Michael was in 1955 given the RHS's highest award, the FCC, and named in honour of my wife 'Elisabeth Holman'.

Magor was a rhododendron man who corresponded over many years with JC, comparing the performance of Forrest's new species; some of their letters have been published and exhibit the deep love of plants of the two correspondents. Magor raised some first-class hybrids; two of the best "blue" rhododendrons, 'St Breward' and 'St Tudy', were raised at Lamellen.

The other member of the trio was George Johnstone, who created one of the world's great shrub gardens at Trewithen. I know of no better planting than that which lines the great glade running south from the house. Two of Forrest's introductions are notable in the garden today; *Magnolia mollicomata* by the glade has few rivals, and the planting of *Pieris forrestii* by the Walled Garden is a fitting memorial to the brilliant collector. The finest rhododendron at Trewithen, however, was collected by Frank Kingdon-Ward in Manipur and given to George Johnstone by Colonel E H W Bolitho of Trengwainton. The rhododendron was *R. macabeanum*.

Although Kingdon-Ward (1885-1958) first joined Forrest in North-west China, Forrest resented this poaching and Ward moved to the west, concentrating on unexplored areas of Northern Burma, Assam, Manipur and Tibet. Colonel Bolitho took a large share of Ward's

expedition in 1926 – introductions from this expedition "made" Trengwainton, just as those of Forrest "made" Caerhays. The fact that the best form of *R. macabeanum* raised at Trengwainton was given to George Johnstone typifies the generosity of gardeners. These tremendous introductions grown by able and passionate gardeners such as those above were to transform Cornish gardens into the outstanding examples we see today.

Despite an occasional failure, the Cornish garden is blessed by its climate. The introductions from China and the East, from North and South America, are today joined by many Australasian species; few of our woodland gardens are without a grove of the Australian tree fern *Dicksonia antarctica* to excite the envy of those who garden in colder climes. In Tresco, agapanthus from South Africa grows like a weed, and other plants flourish which are too tender for the mainland.

The summer of 1995 was hot: very hot, and dry. I have a number of new species from Mexico which all loved this unusual weather for Cornwall. I find this stimulating, and I am excited with the remarkable performance of some of these new species. *Magnolia dealbata*, for instance, raised from seed at Lanhydrock in 1987 and given to Chyverton in 1988, is already 20ft high (6.15m) and flowered at four years, the first time in the open in Europe.

Maybe, with global warming, Cornwall will become another Tresco and, as we go into the next millennium, who knows what the future will bring?

Nigel Holman

Champion Trees – old and new

The term "champion trees" originated as a result of the late Alan Mitchell's sterling work on the largest, fattest, tallest trees he found in the British Isles.

Cornwall has its fair share of such specimens and has had trees of especial note since early times. The Celtic peoples had particular reverence for trees, in particular the oak and oak groves. Even today, people still touch wood to ward off misfortune, a relic of the days when guardian spirits were supposed to live in trees; touching the tree was both a mark of respect for the spirit and a plea for good fortune. The Cornish place name 'kelli' (or grove), as in Kelliwith, the legendary fortress of King Arthur, is still to be found throughout the county even though most of the tree cover has now disappeared. Sacred trees often grew over sacred springs, water being equally important, and remnants of this belief are apparent at a number of wells such as St Keyne's where four different trees (oak, willow, ash and elder) grew magically out of the same root; and others where gnarled and ancient thorns grow above the well. The trees were often decorated with offerings, still to be seen in some countries where Christian saints have taken over the guardianship of healing wells.

The Trebursye oak

The menhir at Dry Tree on Goonhilly Downs being re-erected in 1929

Faint echoes of former tree worship can be found in the festivals that are still celebrated today – the Furry or Floral Dance at Helston is a relict of the May festival when revellers are garlanded with flowers and carry sycamore branches. Greenery and flowers are also carried for the 'Obby Oss' ritual at Padstow and the silver ball for the Hurling game at St Columb Major is made of apple wood. A later tradition, Oak Apple Day on 29th May, commemorating the Royalist cause, is celebrated at St Neot where an oak branch is placed on top of the church tower.

Few large and ancient trees still exist today, the Trebursye oak being a shadow of its former self and the Great Elm of Rosuic (originally with a girth of 26 feet) having succumbed to Dutch Elm Disease (although the latter is, encouragingly, putting forth new shoots). The Darley Oak at Linkinghorne still flourishes however; thought to be over 1,000 years old, it loses a branch from time to time and the tea-house inside is no more, but it is still revered by its owners and passers-by alike.

An extremely large fig tree can be found growing out of the church wall at Manaccan and is considered to be over 200 years old. Another site of interest, also on the Lizard, is the 'Dry Tree' on the Goonhilly Downs. It is not known what sort of tree this was, or even the reason for its fame. It may however have been important due to its location at the meeting point of five parishes, or because of the prehistoric menhir (standing stone) nearby. (Interestingly, the Lizard was once referred to as 'terra arida' or 'dry land', referring to its treeless nature. Perhaps Dry Tree is a derivative of this.)

The treeless Lizard formerly contained another tree of note – the Cury Great Tree, a large ash – which was on the site of a factional fight between

The last tree in England at Lands End c. 1900

The Last Tree in England, Lands End, Cornwall

the men of neighbouring parishes quarelling over the share of booty from smuggling.

Champion trees of the Present Day

Most trees of note today are to be found within large estates and have been planted since the 18th century. Plant hunters such as Douglas and Lobb sent back large quantities of new and exciting species, some of which have now reached an amazing size. With regard to size, there is a well-known saying amongst the gardeners of the county to the effect that "in Cornwall, all trees are shrubs and all shrubs are trees!" A particularly apt example of this is the very large New Zealand tree *Podocarpus totara* at Heligan which has been described in gardening literature as being capable of growing to the size of a shrub in Britain!

The great storm of 1990 had a devastating effect on some of these specimens; the majority, however, still survive. Many conifers had their tops blown out, but the relatively tender magnolias seemed to survive unscathed.

Caerhays garden has the most listed champions, followed closely by Tregrehan. The former has mainly broadleaved species, in particular oaks and magnolias, whilst the latter has an unrivalled collection of conifers.

Although space is too limited to list the trees individually, particular note can be made of the beautiful magnolias at Caerhays, the cork oaks at Mount Edgcumbe and Antony, and the *Cryptomeria japonica* Lobbii from Lobb's original seed at Boconnoc. Trebah has its 50′ (15m) Chusan palms and there are fine examples of *Eucryphia cordifolia* at Trewithen and Trengwainton.

Further information can be found in "Champion Trees of the British Isles" and the article by David Hunt 'Cornish Garden' magazine, March 1992.

Sue Pring

Orchards in Cornwall

Although many people do not associate Cornwall with fruit growing, a long tradition nevertheless exists, dating back to early times.

Apples

The Celtic peoples of the west had a particular reverence for the apple, which features in many of their tales and legends; their Otherworld was set with apple trees on which magical birds would feed and at a later period the legendary King Arthur was taken to Avalon (the Island of Apples) to recover from his wounds. Aval is the Cornish word for apple and place names can still be found based on this - for example, Nansavallan near Truro.

The first detailed written references to apples and orchards are to be found in the Glebe Terriers from the 17th century in which listings were made in order to ascertain how much the glebe (church) land was worth. Details of the number and type of fruit trees were given and also of the presence of cider houses, cider being the universal drink at that period.

All villages would have had their local orchards, but production for commercial purposes was located in the deep drowned river valleys of the south – the Tamar, Fowey and Fal – which both gave shelter and provided an easy means of transport by water.

Many different varieties of apple evolved, with strange and wonderful names. Some described their shape, as in 'Pig's Nose' and 'Bottle Stopper'; others were named after their place of origin – 'Manaccan Primrose' and 'Treloweth Pippin', or their originator – 'Snell's Glass Apple' or 'Ben's Red'. Of particular fame were 'Cornish Gillyflower' or 'Jellyflower', perhaps a corruption of July flower, and the 'Cornish Aromatic', both developed in the

Cornish Gillyflower

Land Army girls picking apples, 1917

early 19th century. General dialect terms also developed such as 'crumpling' – a little, knotty wrinkled apple, 'kerns' – pippins, and 'apple-bee' – a wasp. The tradition of wassailing was common throughout the county and many of the farm workers would gather together to beat the trees and chant wassail songs to improve the next year's crop.

It was not only the labourer who had an orchard attached to his dwelling. The majority of gentlemen's residences of the late 18th and the 19th century grew many varieties. In 1840 the Fox family at Glendurgan were growing 78 varieties of apple alone, in addition to pears and other fruit.

Great care was taken with the harvesting and storing of the fruit, and fruit houses were specially constructed on many estates, detailed specifications being given regarding their construction and usage. For example, at Killiow, near Truro, in the late 19th century, the fruit was not to be stored on slats made of elm, fir or pine (the latter would impart a resinous flavour to the fruit) and the choicest apples were to be wrapped in thin paper and stored in barrels of chaff, sand or powdered charcoal. Although most fruit houses have disappeared, small disused stores can sometimes be seen in walled

Apple picking by **Harold Harvey of the Newlyn School of painters**

gardens, and a reconstructed fruit store based on an original 19th century design can be seen at Heligan Gardens.

Cider

The process of pressing and fermenting apples has gone on for centuries, its origins lost in antiquity. However, cider making was begun in a serious manner by Lord Scuddamore in the 17th century in Hereford, and spread outwards to Devon and Cornwall. Specific cider apples such as 'Redstreak', 'Slap-me-Girdle' and 'Rack-me-down' were bred to give a sweet juice and acid pulp.

Borlase, in 1794, was of the firm opinion that "the constant use of cyder... hath been found by experience to avail much of health and long life... preserving the drinker... in the full strength and vigour even to very old age".

To make the cider, the apples were packed between layers of straw in wooden presses, like enormous many-tiered sandwiches; when pressure was applied the juice drained into the granite base. Another alternative was to use a pony-turned cider mill.

Some surprising additions were made, the Cornish having an aptitude for adding the blood of a sheep or even a whole cockerel. Once in the cask, another even more amazing tradition was sometimes followed – one 19th century writer refers to "one of those old fashioned people who always put a toad into a cask of cider". It was said that toads would sometimes live for twenty years in the ferment; when the cask was empty the creature would be tipped out of the bunghole and people would exclaim "Mind the toad, mind the toad, save 'un up for the next brewen!"

Cherries

In the far east of Cornwall, along the sheltered Tamar valley, the black Tamar cherries known as mazzards were grown. In 1796 the agronomist William Marshall found the area in the vicinity of Cotehele to be "where cherries, pears and walnuts are raised in great abundance for local markets" and estimated that "all of a thousand pounds worth of fruit including strawberries was sent out annually".

In the early days, most of the fruit was sent down river from the many quays along the Tamar, but the arrival of the railways in the mid-19th century opened up new markets and new orchards were soon to replace the woodland.

The cherry orchards themselves are thought to date from the Elizabethan period and a number of different varieties arose including the Brandy Mazzard, said to be similar to a German variety, and many others which were named after the farm where they were first raised. Cultivation was no easy matter; the soil would wash down the steep slopes and had to be carted back up again, and the 45-foot cherry ladders which were often required on the downhill side of the trees needed two strong men to handle them. Under the trees were grown a variety of crops including bulbs, strawberries and gooseberries.

The beautiful orchards in bloom became a tourist attraction; day trippers would arrive packed into river steamers from Plymouth to view the blossom and later in the season to indulge in strawberry teas and cherry pie picnics.

A Tamar cherry orchard

Kea Plums at Cowlands Creek

dredging, fishing, coppicing and fruit cultivation.

Although apples were grown, it is for plums that the area became famous, so much so that 19th century trippers from Truro and Falmouth would come by steamer to buy the plums and take tea. Boats were also used to transport the produce to Truro and Falmouth; a particular type of small sailing boat was used in this area, being a multi-purpose vessel for both fishing and transport.

A number of different plums evolved, including the Kea black, red and grey plums and also the tiny round yellow Crystal Gage and Kestins.

Possibly derived from the wild bullace (or bullum in Cornish dialect) they were developed over the centuries to become specific to the area. Other local plums are the Manaccan plum and the Portscatho plum, both similar to the Kea Black.

Most of the Kea fruit was used for jam making, and during the middle years of this century a jam and canning factory was opened. It only flourished for a few years, however, most of the fruit being sold locally or taken to the jam factory at Truro.

Plums

In contrast to the Tamar cherry orchards were the plum gardens of the upper reaches of the River Fal. Plums have been cultivated since the sixteenth century on the sheltered slopes surrounding the hamlets of Coombe and Kea, where the cottagers made their living from several occupations – oyster

Plum Gardens at Combe Creek

Pears

Pears were also grown, mainly in the sheltered walled gardens of the larger residences, where a wide range of predominantly French varieties were cultivated. Although the aristocracy produced pears mainly for dessert, an interesting reference to Trevithick, St Ewe, indicates that in 1726 the pears were probably being used to produce perry – a sparkling drink akin to cider.

100-year-old vines at Trevarno

The Plymouth pear, Britain's rarest tree, survives at only two wild sites in the country, one in Cornwall and one in Devon. Today the tree is restricted to hedgerows but is thought to have originally been a component of natural oak woodlands.

The tree produces a spectacular display of pink-tinged blossom but the fruits are very small and inedible. Due to its scarcity, English Nature has included it in a Species Recovery Programme in order to safeguard the existing population and re-establish the tree in suitable localities. A specimen of the tree can be seen in the Fruit Collection at Trelissick, where the species is being propagated to ensure its survival.

The Plymouth pear (*Pyrus cordata*)

Vines and Vineyards

Today only a small handful of vineyards can be found in the county. This limited number seems to have been the case since records began and it is only the fact that there are a number of vineyard names on maps and in lease agreements that gives any indication that they ever existed. There appears to be no written confirmation of this in Tithe returns or other accounts. Eighteenth century vineyard names appear in Truro, Gulval and Gwennap and others from as far back as the 16th century near Penryn. Although climatic change may indicate that conditions are less suitable today, it is unlikely that an eminently drinkable wine was regularly produced from the grapes. Instead, verjuice (a type of vinegar) common in medieval and Tudor times, would have been the most likely product.

In West Penwith, the far west of Cornwall, where vineyard names have also been found, it is thought that the derivation is from "vinack", from the Cornish for stony, the fields being very stony and also small and apparently unsuitable for growing grapes.

There is, however, one substantiated reference at Land's End, where in the 1880s a vineyard with the grapes in four large vinehouses, one 220 feet long, was developed by a Mr Boddy. Quite how the glasshouses survived in the teeth of the Atlantic gales is a mystery – there is no reference to the vineyard's demise or how long it existed.

A selection of Cornish apple varieties

The 19th century also saw the upsurge of interest by the gentry in the cultivation of many varieties of grape. These had care and attention lavished on them by an army of gardeners whose job it was to regulate the vinehouse temperature at all hours of the day and night, and to prune, thin and pick the grapes.

Few of these beautiful vineries exist today and even fewer have the same amount of care. The armies of gardeners have passed into memory and only the crumbling glasshouses remain, with a few vines valiantly striving against the weather and time. The way of life has disappeared forever and only faint echoes can be seen in gardens such as Trevarno where magnificent old vines still flourish, and at Heligan where restoration has taken place.

Key to apple varieties

1. BEN'S RED	6. GRAMPOUND PIPPIN
2. CORNISH AROMATIC	7. SYDNEY STRAKE
3. CORNISH PINE	8. CORNISH GILLIFLOWER (TRURO)
4. WARLEGGAN WASSAIL	9. VERYAN PIPPIN
5. CORNISH QUARENDON	10. CORNISH GILLIFLOWER (LAUNCESTON)

The Cornish Orchard Project

As can be seen from the above, many orchards have long disappeared and fruit growing as an industry has almost become extinct.

At the eleventh hour, however, Cornwall County Council has initiated a project for the restoration of old orchards and the planting of new ones using old varieties. At present 56 old varieties are being grown, budded onto M25 and M111 rootstocks, which at a year old are being sold at an advantageous rate to interested landowners. Four varieties of cherry have also been grown and supplied to the Tamar area. The project supports both large and small schemes ranging from 10 trees to 250. Demonstration collections have been set up and Apple Days held where fruit can be brought for identification – the first, held in 1991 at Probus Demonstration Garden, was very successful and has led to a number of varieties being re-discovered which were hitherto thought to be lost.

A number of varieties that grow on their own stocks were also identified. Known locally as 'pitchers' they root naturally at the crooks of the branches; it was common practice to break a piece off and 'pitch' it into the ground to produce a new tree.

Collections of Cornish fruit can be seen at Catchfrench, Lanhydrock, Heligan, Dairyland, Trelissick and Trerice, and further information on the project can be obtained from the County Forester at County Hall, Truro.

Sue Pring

Commercial Horticulture in Cornwall

The production of cut flowers in Cornwall started towards the end of the 19th century when the new railways facilitated quick and easy access to London's Covent Garden. The west of Cornwall and the Isles of Scilly were to become the centre of flower production, in particular of daffodils – so much so that by the turn of the century 60 million blooms were being exported from the Isles of Scilly alone.

Although it is thought that narcissi have been growing on the islands for hundreds of years, having been brought by the Benedictine monks to Tresco Abbey, it was not until 1871 that William Trevellick of St Mary's sent a hat box of daffodils to Covent Garden for which he received the princely sum of seven shillings and sixpence.

Shortly afterwards, the "King" of Scilly, T A Dorien-Smith, had the foresight to realize that the frost-free climate of the islands was perfectly suited to the raising of early flowers. He encouraged the islanders to shelter their fields with hedges of pittosporum, euonymous, hebe and escallonia, and he also travelled extensively in Belgium and Holland searching out up to 190 new varieties of narcissus.

Many beautiful and scented varieties were grown, most famous of all being the yellow 'Soleil d'Or' and the lovely 'Paper White'. The bulbs were grown in rows six to nine inches apart in specially prepared beds, well manured with easily available seaweed.

The industry also expanded to include other bulbs including ixias, lilies, anemones, arums and "whistling jacks", the latter being the intensely bright cerise *Gladiolus communis subs. byzantinus*. Many of these former crops have now naturalized throughout the island, some in the most inhospitable of places; agapanthus can even be seen growing right next to the shore in places.

An extensive breeding programme for bulbs was also carried out; first at Gulval in the 1920s and then following the Second World War at Rosewarne Experimental Station. Developments at Rosewarne included the valuable cold-resistant strains of 'St Piran' anemone and a range of hybrid lilies.

Two private individuals were also heavily involved in their own breeding programmes for daffodils, P D Williams of Lanarth and J C

Packing daffodils at Woodcock's farm, St Mary's, Scilly

Williams of Caerhays. The variety 'Carlton', registered at Lanarth in 1927, still occupies more land than any other variety.

The industry has remained an important one, with air transport now being used from Scilly, and was even carried on throughout the Second World War, in spite of many fields having been converted to food crops and a ban on the export of flowers. Shortly after the ban was imposed, when Winston Churchill was in hospital, Scillonians sent him a large box of daffodils along with wishes for a speedy recovery. Churchill responded by allowing a quota to be introduced, and the demand for flowers during the hard times of war became enormous. Prices rose and the smuggling of flowers became commonplace, using all manner of subterfuges including the RAF rescue service and even a coffin!

On the mainland too, flowers were an important industry. Tiny box-like fields enclosed in sheltering dry stone Cornish hedges were cultivated on the sharply sloping cliffs of Mounts Bay. There fishermen, miners and others would grow violets and anemones for sale and their fields feature in paintings by the Lamorna and Newlyn Schools of artists.

From the sea the fishermen setting out at dawn could watch the sunrise light cliffs of colour as spectacular as any cultivated garden, and in calm weather the scent of violet and narcissus from the shore would brighten the start of the day. Before the advent of weed killers, flower farmers clearing a bulb field for a different variety would dig up the old crop and toss the bulbs into the nearby hedges

Scilly Whites

and woods. Now, in wooded valleys such as Boskenna and Lamorna and in the hedgerows, daffodils grow and spread like bluebells. With daffodil bulbs available cheaply in quantity in Cornwall, local authorities have planted them in golden drifts beside the new roads that by-pass many towns, giving spring pleasure to the people of Cornwall and their visitors.

Sue Pring and Daphne Lawry

Cutting cauliflowers (known confusingly as broccoli in Cornwall) at Marazion c. 1950

Gazetteer

Antony, Torpoint

The earliest feature to survive at Antony is Richard Carew's 'fishful pond'. A scholar and antiquary, whose greatest and lasting achievement was his "Survey of Cornwall" published in 1602, he wrote in detail of the construction and workings of his salt water pond.

The first illustrations of the gardens in 1727 were by Edmund Prideaux who depicted an astonishing array of tree-lined avenues and formal parterres to the north of the house. Although Prideaux's drawing of the south front shows the perfectly proportioned house with pavilions and arcades, it does not show the wall and gates which were added later to enclose the south side of the forecourt.

The next phase in the development of the garden took place at the end of the 18th century when Reginald Pole-Carew sought the advice of Humphry Repton. For 30 guineas Repton produced one of his famous Red Books which so delighted his client that he wrote "I was up to twelve at night, and could not go to sleep until I thoroughly examined the treasure you put in my hands".

Repton, in his usual style, suggested that the formal parterres and kitchen garden must go in order to create uninterrupted vistas to the river, and the enclosing wall to the south forecourt should be opened up to increase the initial impact. Although the former suggestion was taken up and a new kitchen garden built, the south forecourt remained unaltered. Plantations were also laid out by Pole-Carew with Repton's advice in mind. The next contribution was by William Henry Pole-Carew who added new plantations, and is thought to have planted the yew hedges lining the terrace to the west.

William's son, Reginald, was particularly active in garden making during the late 19th and in the early 20th century. He restored the 18th-century parterres, framed the view of the river with a

The formal yew walk at Antony House

wrought iron screen and gates, extended the yew walk and closed the vista with an enormous Burmese bell, whilst at the same time renewing the ageing plantations.

The early 20th century saw further garden activity under the auspices of Sir John and Lady Carew Pole. Inspired by the rhododendrons at Exbury they planted many species and hybrids which flourished in the surrounding woodlands. Camellias and Asiatic magnolias were also planted at this time.

As with most country house gardens, after the Second World War the garden was greatly simplified, with labour intensive features such as the Victorian parterres and flower beds being replaced with grass. However, more recent development of the garden has seen the creation of the Summer Garden and Knot Garden, both designed by the then Mrs Mary (now Lady) Carew Pole in the 1980s. These two delightful gardens feature shrubs, herbaceous perennials and scented herbs.

Of a number of walks, the Yew Walk is the oldest and contains a beautiful stone seat flanked by two charming 18th-century statues. The other walks are the Magnolia and Lilac Walks, the former with *Magnolia denudata* providing a wonderful show of white flowers early in the spring.

The northern terraces overlook the main lawn with clumps of *Quercus ilex* on either side framing the view of the River Lynher. The terraces themselves feature mixed shrubs and herbaceous plantings with roses and ceanothus. An early 18th century dovecote lies at the end of the terraces. Eggs were collected by means of a revolving potence with three layers of platforms on a central elm trunk support.

To the east of the house lies the Oriental Pond with associated plantings of *Acer palmatum dissectum* and wisteria. In contrast, the Courtyard on the south front retains its formality with planting restricted to the walls where the evergreen *Magnolia grandiflora* 'Exmouth' scents the summer air. Also in this area can be seen the National Collection of Hemerocallis (Day Lilies). Over 500 cultivars have been collected, including some developed at Antony such as 'Sir John' and 'Antony House'.

Finally, to the west of the house is the Cork Oak lawn containing an immense cork oak (*Quercus suber*) and fruiting shrubs and trees, including mulberries, walnuts and *Cornus capitata*.

Location: Antony House, Torpoint
Tel: National Trust (01752) 812 191
Facilities: Disabled Access, Teas, Toilets, No Dogs, Car & Coach Park, Guide book.

Antony Woodland Garden, Torpoint

This garden, owned by the Carew Pole Charitable Trust, adjoins the National Trust Gardens and is divided into two areas, each with its own distinctive character. To the west can be found the Jupiter Wilderness and the West Down woodlands.

This part of the garden is laid out in a more formal setting partly based on Repton's lay-out of 1793 with views over the house and river. In the vicinity of Jupiter Point are massed old hybrid rhododendrons and azaleas, whilst at the "cross roads" may be seen groups of magnolias and Japanese acers.

A series of ponds filled with water lilies lead towards the Bath Pond and Bath House. The Bath House, built between 1788 and 1790, is partially roofed over in the style of a Roman atrium. The pond was used as a plunge bath and is, unusually, filled with sea water, fed via the adjacent pond from the River Lynher. Other interesting features nearby are the remnants of salt pans where salt was produced for agricultural purposes.

The West Down woodlands were largely planted after the Second World War and include many fine specimens of magnolia and camellia.

Progressing further towards the Higher West Down wood, one passes through the Garden Field where varieties of birch are under-planted with

The 18th century bath house at Antony Woodland Garden

drifts of daffodils. Passing along the Camellia Walk one reaches the turning point of the path where wild primroses and violets can be seen in the spring as ground cover to the extensive camellia collection.

To the east of the car park, paths lead through woods and parkland towards an enclosed estuarine inlet designed in the 16th century by Richard Carew and know as his Fishful Pond. He was so passionate about this achievement, he not only gave detailed explanation of its construction, but was also inspired to write:-

> *"Where sucking millet, swallowing basse,*
> *Side walking crab, wry mouthed flook*
> *And slip fist eel, as evenings pass,*
> *For safe bait at due place to look*
> *Bold to approach, quick to espy,*
> *Greedy to catch, ready to fly.*
> *In heat the top, in cold the deep*
> *In Spring the month, the winds in neap*
> *With changeless change by shoals they keep*
> *Fat, fruitful, ready but not cheap*
> *Thus mean in state, and calm in sprite*
> *My fishful pond is my delight."*
> (Carew's Survey of Cornwall, 1602)

The pond contained crustaceans and various sea fish such as mullet, bass and whiting.

Also in this section of the garden are the remains of an ancient dovecote. Wilder areas with drifts of bluebells and snowdrops can be admired in this part of the woodland garden, whilst taking in the excellent views over the surrounding countryside.

Location: Near Antony House, Antony Road, Torpoint
Tel: (01752) 814 210
Facilities: Part Disabled Access, Toilets (N.T.),
No Dogs, Car Park.
(National Trust toilets available on open days only)

Barbara Hepworth Museum, St Ives

Trewyn Studio stands at the bottom of Barnoon Hill, a short walk away from the hustle and bustle of the centre of St Ives. Although unremarkable from the outside behind its high walls of granite blocks, this enclosed garden is a haven of tranquillity. In 1949 the sculptress Barbara Hepworth bought the house and land at auction and it was her studio for two years until she moved in permanently, remaining until her death in 1975. Her sculpture workshops are left in the same condition as they were on the day she died, with unfinished works, tools, her assistants' overalls hanging on their pegs, and everything looking as though, at any moment, she might walk through the door and pick up where she left off.

She planned the lay-out of the garden and selected many plants to provide a setting for her astonishing sculptures. Still existing are her plantings of a number of substantial trees including *Gingko biloba*, flowering cherries, metasequoia and cordylines, with large shrubs such as camellia, myrtle and ceanothus and ground cover plants of woodruff, geranium and lungwort.

The Barbara Hepworth Sculpture Garden

One of the special features of the garden was the large clumps of cineraria (*Senecio cruentus*) which were naturalized in the garden for many years, resulting in relatively hardy forms and providing a gentle background of pastel shades of blue, mauve and pink.

Location: Barnoon Hill, St Ives
Tel: (01736) 796 226
(Administered by The Tate Gallery, St Ives)
[The adjacent Trewyn Gardens, which before 1949 was part of the garden of Trewyn House, is a public garden in the ownership of Penwith District Council and has a well kept selection of tender shrubs and mature trees.]

Boconnoc, Lostwithiel

The Deer Park at Boconnoc is the oldest surviving example in Cornwall, dating back to medieval times. Ancient trees are still to be found here, covered in a fine assemblage of mosses and lichens which flourish in the clean Cornish air, many of them planted by the Mohun family who owned the estate during the 16th century.

The woodland garden at Boconnoc

The "Picturesque" landscape, however, dates mainly from the 18th century when Thomas Pitt purchased Boconnoc with one half of the proceeds from the famous Pitt diamond. (Whilst Governor of Madras in 1719, he had purchased the diamond for £20,400. Although £5,000 was expended in cutting, the chips alone were sold for £8,000 and the diamond itself for an astounding £135,000!)

Most of the landscaping was carried out by his descendant, the 1st Lord Camelford, during the late 18th century. He constructed a number of classical features including two shrines, a stone bathing pool and an obelisk, and laid out large plantations both to protect the house from prevailing winds and to enhance the view. Today from the house, set in the centre of the estate in a secluded wooded valley, magnificent views are obtained over the park and down the Lerryn valley.

The gardens, of approximately 20 acres, the bones of which were laid out by the 1st Lord Camelford, can now be divided into four sections: The Dorothy Gardens, the Shrubbery, the Stewardry Walk and the Lawns and Rockery by Boconnoc House (now sadly derelict).

On arrival, visitors first enter the Dorothy Garden, named after the great-grandmother of the present owner. The centre of the Dorothy Garden contains a pretty fountain; also in this garden is a fine plane tree together with tulip trees, yews, azaleas, a huge *Eucryphia x nymansensis*, camellias, rhododendrons and other plantings by the present owners. Beyond this, the shrubbery contains a rare Japanese umbrella pine (*Sciadopitys verticillata*), a lily pond surrounded by Japanese azaleas, camellias, rhododendrons and many more acid-loving shrubs.

Before entering the Stewardry Walk, an old quarry filled with Japanese azaleas can be seen on the left. The Stewardry Walk is characterised by more rhododendrons, azaleas and camellias, and contains an unusual waterfall surrounded by palms, primulas and other water loving plants. From here there is a magnificent view over the river Lerryn of the "Valley Crucis". The cross, visible in the distance, stands on top of spoil removed from an adit in the nearby lead mine and was placed there by G M Fortescue in memory of his uncle, Lord Grenville, in 1840.

The house itself was requisitioned during the last war, and both house and estate were used extensively by American troops in the build-up to the Normandy invasion.

Behind the rockery on the east side of the house is Boconnoc Church, a fine mainly 15th century building which strangely had no original tower, the present short bell tower being constructed by G M Fortescue in the 1850s. Church services are still held here every Sunday and visitors can purchase a brief history of Boconnoc and the church in the church itself. (Key available from the Estate Office.)

[The Estate and Gardens are all private but the Gardens are open in the spring for different charities.]

Location: Boconnoc, Lostwithiel – south of A390 near W Taphouse
Tel: (01208) 872 507
Facilities: Part Disabled Access, Teas, Toilets, Plant Sales, Dogs on leads, Car & Coach Park.

Bosahan, Manaccan

This five-acre valley garden is situated on the south bank of the beautiful Helford River. Uniquely, it covers not one valley but two, and consequently has more sheltered spots for tender treasures than many other Cornish gardens. The depth of the valleys together with substantial planting of tree screens over the upper valley side shelter it from the north east.

Although a dwelling has been on the site since the 16th century, the current lay-out of the gardens largely dates from the early 19th century, when the house became the home of the Grylls family followed by the Graham-Vivians.

The walls of the demolished Victorian Gothic mansion have been preserved to enclose a court-yard garden to the rear of the existing house, whilst formal terraces planted with laurels to the east of the house are also remnants of an earlier scheme.

The valley gardens contain many unusual species. In the western valley, running down to Pedgagarack Cove, is the Fern Glen with its series of pools set amongst tree ferns and a profusion of other moisture loving species. Of particular note are the fine Royal ferns (*Osmunda regalis*).

The garden at the head of the Big Wood valley falls to the palm fringed fish pond and contains the main area of choice shrub planting. In addition to splendid azaleas, magnolias and rhododendrons there are substantial plantings of New Zealand trees and shrubs and there is a lovely patch of native spring flowers and young silver birch trees towards the pond. The majority of specimen trees are to be found at the head of Big Wood valley, with fine examples of sequoia and taxodium with an under-storey of Japanese maples, Chusan palms and myrtles. Ornamental pheasants roam free about the garden.

Location: Manaccan, Helston
Tel: (01326) 231 330
Facilities: Part Disabled Access, Teas, Toilets,
Dogs on leads, Car & Coach Park.
N.B. Parking in field if dry – otherwise hard surface at farm. Coaches park at farm.

Bosvigo, Truro

Bosvigo differs from most other Cornish gardens in many ways. Firstly, it isn't an old garden – some of it is fifteen years old but much is younger and is still being developed and improved year by year. Another big difference is its location – it doesn't have a wonderful valley sloping down to the sea but stands not far from the centre of Truro, whose suburbs have expanded and surrounded it. By far the biggest difference is that it is not a spring garden; there are no great drifts of rare rhododendron and camellias are not great favourites here, but a few deciduous azaleas are tolerated for their brief flowers in exchange for their superb scent and the wonderful autumn colours. The emphasis at Bosvigo is on herbaceous plants which are chosen carefully to give a steady succession of colour and texture throughout the summer.

The walled garden at Bosvigo

Many separate areas have been created around the delightful Georgian house (not open) to create a series of "garden rooms", each with its own colour theme. The Walled Garden is a quiet, refined symphony of pinks, blues and purples. Many varieties of old-fashioned roses decorate the walls, with clematis and ornamental vines threading their way amongst them.

A Victorian conservatory now stands isolated from the house – a large and ugly wing was demol-ished to restore the Georgian symmetry. It is planted with a variety of climbers which give scent and colour all through the summer. Seats are provided to entice the visitor to sit and relax for a while in this delightful setting. Other gardens have different colour themes – the Vean garden is mainly gold and white, with a touch of blue here and there. The Pink and Grey garden speaks for itself. The Green and Black bed is full of strange plants, such as the green rose. The Hot garden is planted with shrieking reds, yellows and oranges, all held in check (well, almost!) by the use of much purple foliage.

On the site of the old tennis court is a small nursery selling a wide range of the herbaceous plants that make the garden so magnificent.

Location: Off A390 (Truro to Redruth) at Highertown first right after Sainsbury roundabout – down Dobbs Lane, 500 yards on left
Tel and fax: (01872) 75774
Facilities: Part Disabled Access, Toilets, Plant Sales (Catalogue), No Dogs, Car Park.

Burncoose Nurseries and Garden, Gwennap

Burncoose is a garden created by the famous Williams family. Although the estate was first purchased in 1715, the development of the garden was initiated by John Williams (IV) during the first half of the 19th century. Here, as at most Cornish gardens, the Victorian passion for new introductions was embraced. The next influence would have been the Rogers family, Mrs Powys Rogers being the sister of the Caerhays Williams, who introduced many trees and shrubs from Caerhays. After a period of neglect during the Second World War the garden is now being brought back to its former glory. A setback occurred owing to the great storm in 1990 when hundreds of trees were blown down. As elsewhere, this tragedy has been turned to advantage, with several thousand trees and shrubs

Bluebells at Burncoose

being planted in the spaces created. Whilst carrying out the new planting the owner has been careful not to spoil the charming carpets of bluebells, primroses and wild violets which grow in abundance in late winter and spring. From one of the bluebell glades can be seen flamboyant groups of evergreen azaleas adjacent to the house.

At the bottom of the garden is a peaceful pool surrounded by mature Japanese maples with graceful clumps of bamboo dating from the "bamboo craze" of the late 19th century.

A small walled and hedged garden to the back of the house has been replanted with more exotic plants such as phormiums and ceanothus which, it was felt, would have been alien to the woodland garden.

The rest of the large walled gardens have been used to accommodate a series of tunnels in which are grown the thousands of plants produced by the renowned nursery business. Of particular interest in this section are a number of Chinese gooseberry or Kiwi fruit *(Actinidia deliciosa)* which line the old walls and produce a good crop of fruit.

A number of plants raised at Burncoose can be seen in the gardens – these include *Magnolia sprengeri diva* 'Burncoose' – a striking reddish purple – and *Camellias* 'Burncoose Apple Blossom' and 'Monica Dance'.

Location: Gwennap, Redruth on A393
Tel: (01209) 861 112
Facilities: Disabled Access, Tea Rooms, Toilets, Plant Sales, Catalogue, Dogs on leads, Car & Coach Park.

Caerhays Castle Garden, St Austell

Caerhays, the ultimate in romantic '"Gothic" fantasy castles, lies cradled in a small valley overlooking the sea at Porthluney Cove. The castle was designed by Nash for the Trevanions during the early years of the 19th century, and it is thought that Repton might have been consulted about the landscaping. Unfortunately John Trevanion's finances were insufficient to support such a grandiose scheme and by 1840 the money had run out, Trevanion escaping his creditors by fleeing to Paris.

In 1864 the castle, by this time in a deplorable state with no roof, was purchased by the Williams family. Enormously wealthy, due to their mining interests, they restored the castle and were able to take up residence in 1864 when they began work on the gardens, too late for the first influx of rhododendrons from Hooker's expeditions.

The gardens as seen today began to take their present form in 1896 when J C Williams retired from politics to indulge his passion for gardening. Although initially interested in daffodil hybridizing, he had the foresight to support plant exploration; in particular by E H Wilson and George Forrest. From the early 1900s until 1926 Caerhays became one of the distribution centres for new plants sent back by these most famous of plant hunters. Material from the plant hunters was raised at Werrington and then the more tender plants went to Caerhays and the hardier ones stayed at Werrington where another branch of the Williams family lives. From this period, a number of plants still survive; in particular, *Magnolia campbellii ssp. mollicomata* and *Magnolia veitchii*, the latter having attained great height and girth.

Caerhays Castle

Also introduced by Forrest at that time was *Camellia saluenensis* which, crossed with *C. japonica* by J C Williams during the 1920s, created the form known as *williamsii* hybrids. These new camellias proved to be hardier, more floriferous and vigorous than most camellias growing at that time and led to the widespread introduction of camellias into gardens large and small.

Among the J C Williams hybrids of particular note were the deep pink 'St Ewe' and the white 'Cornish Snow'. J C Williams did not limit himself to camellia hybridization. Rhododendrons were also used, producing the popular 'Blue Tit' (*impeditum x augustinii*) and 'Humming Bird' (*haematodes x williamsianum*).

Nowadays Caerhays continues to be a developing garden. More recent hybridization has produced the *Rhododendron* 'Caerhays Philip' (*cinnabarinum x concatenans*) and the notable *Magnolia* 'Caerhays Surprise'.

The combination of the great storm in 1990, when over 900 trees fell, and the death of plants through old age, has led to many spaces becoming available for the rejuvenation of the garden. Large numbers of plants, including new varieties, continue to be introduced each season.

Whilst looking at the newer and smaller treasures, the visitor must not forget to look upwards. It is possible to walk under the enormous magnolias without noticing they are in flower. To do so could be to miss one of the most stunning sights – enormous pink flowers the size of dinner plates set against a bright blue sky remain one of the wonders of Caerhays and have to be seen to be believed!

Location: West of Gorran, St Austell
Tel: (01872) 501 144
Facilities: Part Disabled Access, Teas, Toilets, Plant Sales, Dogs on leads, Free Car & Coach Park.

Carclew Garden, Truro

The first depiction of the gardens at Carclew is to be found on a fascinating map dating from the mid-18th century. This complex plan shows formal parterres, avenues, serpentine walks and formal pools. Although formal gardens in the vicinity of the main building were aligned towards it, the water gardens to the west were quite separate and could not be seen from the house.

These early developments were by Samuel Kempe who, according to Tonkin in the 18th century, was a profligate rogue who died in 1728 leaving his wife in possession of an unfinished house and garden. Shortly after his death it was bought by William Lemon whose immense fortunes from mining were, in part, from the aptly named "Wheal Fortune" mine.

Borlase's engraving in 1758 shows the house flanked on either side by trees, as built by the first Mr Lemon. It was, however, left to Sir William, his grandson, to improve the grounds by laying out the plantations and woodlands. During this period the first Lucombe oaks (*Quercus x hispanica 'Lucombeana'*) were planted. It is said that the Lucombe who first discovered this evergreen hybrid was a gardener at Carclew before he started his famous nursery in Devon. In view of the fact that Loudon refers to one of these oaks dating from 1764, it is likely that these are some of the first Lucombe oaks to be planted in the county.

The pond garden at Carclew

Sir Charles Lemon, who inherited Carclew in 1824, was an equally keen gardener and it is to him that we owe the wonderful rhododendrons. He was a good friend of Joseph Hooker, and was the recipient of many seeds from the Himalayan expeditions. These he shared with other gardens such as Heligan and Tremough; in exchange they supplied him with other treasures. Interestingly Mrs Lemon, in writing to her daughter Caroline Tremayne at Heligan, spoke of "Nepaul" seeds being received (from an unknown source) as early as 1822. These subsequently grew into the dazzling crimson "Nepaul" rhododendrons so admired by Barclay Fox in 1842.

The garden was supervised in Victorian times by W B Booth, a famous gardener of his time. It was under his auspices that the lovely rhododendron 'Sir Charles Lemon' was raised and the original plant can still be seen in the gardens.

The 19th century also saw the development of the terraced garden to the east of the ponds and the laying out of a formal allée with bedding in a chain pattern to the rear of the house focused on a charming 18th-century neo-Gothic chapel.

Arthur Tremayne, who inherited the property towards the end of the 19th century, was also a keen gardener with a particular passion for Japanese irises and bamboos. However, all this was to be brought to an end with a disastrous fire in 1934 which left the house a ruin and led to the abandonment of both house and garden. (The wonderfully romantic ruin still stands – perhaps more beautiful in death than it had ever been in life.)

The property was sold, with the major part of the gardens centred around the old ponds being divided from the main house; and the gardens became completely overgrown until 1963 when Jack Siley bought the old kitchen gardens and shrubberies surrounding the pool. He built a new house at the top of the walled gardens and proceeded to clear, replant and install some extremely fine statues of mermen in the pool, together with a romantic Grecian style temple overlooking the pool.

Many of the shrubs date from this period and also from the subsequent owners, the late Judge Chope and his family, who have continued to develop the garden.

From the terraces there is a wonderful view over the enormous rhododendrons and camellias with a backdrop of mature beech and oak. Along the old kitchen walls can be seen many tender shrubs planted since the 1960s; these include some fine acers in addition to more exotic tender species.

At the base of the terraces can be seen a fine example of *Camellia* 'Captain Rawes'.

In addition to the large pond, smaller pools are also present in sheltered parts of the garden, which is divided up into a series of compartments based on the old productive gardens.

Location: Perran-ar-Worthal, Truro – off A39 near Perran-ar-Worthal
Tel: (01872) 864 071
Facilities: Teas, No Dogs, Car & Coach Park.

Carwinion, Mawnan Smith

Carwinion is basically an unmanicured wild valley garden lying parallel to Glendurgan and Trebah, and runs down towards the Helford River.

Wild Gardening

Within this plot you may observe
'Tis Nature's balance we conserve.
For who are we to specify
Which plants may live and which must die?
And if the weeds seem thick and rank
Then Nature's bounty we must thank;
Nor think, with over tidy mind,
"The gardeners here must all be blind."

The least disorder in the beds
Is something that the gardener dreads;
But personally we prefer
Those chance effects which may occur
When Nature, in her care-free way,
Hangs some graceful flowering spray
Across the path – exactly where
It gets into the gardener's hair.

Anon.

The garden was created in the 1800s by the great-grandfather of the present incumbent, Anthony Rogers. It covers about 10 acres and is now the home of one of the premier collections of bamboos in the United Kingdom. A collection of ferns is also being established, giving added interest to the plantsman.

The valley holds many sub-tropical plants. Walking underneath the huge leaves of the giant rhubarb (*Gunnera manicata*) in the evening, one almost expects a prehistoric monster to emerge! Amongst the most spectacular plants are a fine Japanese cedar (*Cryptomeria japonica*), probably the finest example of a Tasmanian cedar (*Athrotaxis laxifolia*) in Europe, and two most spectacular tree ferns (*Dicksonia antarctica*).

Around the house there are many camellias and evergreen oaks, and to the south-east is an extremely interesting area of wild blue wood anemones, which were rare even in 1853.

The garden is in the process of being renovated and replanted, in particular the Fern Garden which is located in the quarry on the east side of the valley.

Carwinion House

Location: Mawnan Smith, Falmouth
Tel: (01326) 250 258
Facilities: Part Disabled Access, Teas, Toilets, Plant Sales, Dogs on leads, Car Parking in drive.

Catchfrench Manor Garden, St Germans

There has been a family seat at Catchfrench since the 13th Century, but the earliest documented knowledge is of its rebuilding in 1580 by George Kekewich, following a fire.

Francis Glanville commissioned Rawlinson to remodel the house in 1726 and subsequently took advantage of Humphry Repton's expertise to landscape the park.

Humphry Repton visited Catchfrench in October 1792 and personally laid out many of his proposals on the ground with stakes. He subsequently produced his Red Book for Catchfrench in 1793 detailing further ideas. All his original planting intentions were implemented, plus some subsequent planting after the closure of the main turnpike in 1830. This previously ran through the estate and much of the planting had been implemented to screen the road from the house.

The Knoll was planted using beech, sweet chestnut and oak, in such a way as to reveal the house "at its best point of view" on rounding a bend in the newly created drive from the west. The Knoll was complemented on the opposite side of the drive by a small group of sycamore and holm oak, most of which were unfortunately felled during the war. It is the intention to replant this area in accordance with the Red Book design.

Repton used many of the existing features, enhancing them to make them more "Picturesque". From the straight Elizabethan terrace, running parallel to the Elizabethan house from the walled garden to the Little Knoll, there is an extensive vista.

The Quarry Garden was created by Repton and he suggested that if planted with care it would "furnish an endless source of amusement". This is one of the first areas of the restoration programme, having recently been cleared of overgrown laurels and fallen trees. The next task is to reinstate paths and carry out replanting. The Quarry is indeed a secret garden in that the only access is through a low narrow tunnel, although a viewing platform was provided by Repton at the edge of Quarry Wood.

Other features in the grounds attributed to Repton include sweet chestnuts planted two or three in a hole and non-indigenous rocks at strategic path intersections. Possibly his most significant effect on the landscape at Catchfrench was his radical movement of earth to create a view to a distant cottage on the estate. The earth from this excavation was then used to raise the area in front of the house to reduce its apparent height.

As with most Cornish gardens later plantings include a wealth of magnificent magnolias, rhododendrons, camellias and azaleas, and a number of acers to provide autumn colour.

Nearer to the house, an ancient wisteria is to be found within the courtyard. The walls of the ruin are covered with climbers including species of akebia, *Hydrangea petiolaris*, clematis, etc.

The Elizabethan garden, created on the upper storey of the ruined Elizabethan house, has been laid out and prepared for planting as a herb garden with the intention of including as many of the lesser known and medicinal herbs as possible. The culinary herbs will be in beds edged with box and the garden will be screened by a tall yew hedge which has just been planted. There is also a newly planted rose garden in this area.

During restoration work an interesting Elizabethan drainage system has been revealed which was possibly part of the water system feeding the well in the East Shrubbery. More work will be needed to discover the full extent of the system.

The nearby orchard contains several ancient Cornish varieties of apple.

Location: Catchfrench, St Germans, off A38 5 miles east of Liskeard.
Tel: (01503) 240 759
Facilities: Part Disabled Access, Tea Room, Toilets, Plants on Sale. No Dogs except Guides.
Historical interpretation material.
N.B. Coach park by arrangement.

Churchtown, Morval

Churchtown Gardens were created 34 years ago from the vegetable gardens and old orchards of Morval House. The walled kitchen garden, originally used for fruit growing, dates from 1750 and there was formerly a vinery dating from 1753. Unfortunately the glass house became unsafe and was taken down; however, an old lead trough dated 1753, which was in the vinery, still survives.

The walls of the garden are of brick, unusual at such an early date, and had a coping of thatch (estate accounts record payments to a thatcher).

As can be imagined, it was an enormous task tackling the removal of great laurel hedges, brambles and nettles from the old vegetable area; and the best way found was to do it in sections, clearing the ground with potatoes and then seeding

The Elizabethan doorway at Catchfrench

to make lawns and beds. The last part, the old fowls' runs, was cleared in 1994 and then planted with various eucalyptus, magnolias, camellias and other shrubs. As the soil is unsuitable for acid-loving plants they are all in circular beds with made-up soil. Following generous feeding and plenty of mulching with leaf-mould and peat, the owners have succeeded in growing a lot of azaleas, camellias, magnolias and heathers, etc.

The situation of the garden is interesting as it lies in a dip with a small wood on one side and fields on the other and can be viewed from paths in the wood or the fields. Over more than thirty years the owners have collected and planted millions of snowdrops, both early and late varieties, which in early March are a wonderful sight.

The peaceful atmosphere, remarked on by many people who visit the garden, may be in part due to the closeness of the 13th century Morval Church, St. Wenna. This contrast between old and new is part of the unique charm of this new garden formed on ancient bones.

Location: Morval, Looe – off A374
Tel: (015034) 240 363
Facilities: Disabled Access, Teas, Toilets, No Dogs.
N.B. All parking in lane.

The 'Monet' style bridge at Chyverton

Chyverton, Zelah

The lovely lawns which sweep down to the tranquil lake and elegant stone bridge at Chyverton date from the Georgian period, and were laid out by John Thomas, mine owner, between 1770 and 1820. When he inherited, the only existing woodland was a small copse protecting the house from the prevailing westerlies. He also planted shrubberies and encircling plantations complete with a hill-top folly which was formerly used as a hunting lodge. The productive kitchen garden, at some distance from the house, also dates from this period. Thomas died in 1825 and the estate was inherited by his daughter Frances, the wife of Henry Peter of Harlyn House, Padstow. They first decided to live at Harlyn, and the estate was put on the market in 1833. The sale particulars are in the County Museum and it is interesting to compare them with an estate map of 1770; they show that in the 55 years of his tenure John Thomas planted 94 acres of woodland. The property was not sold, as the Peters decided to live at Chyverton. The house stayed with the Thomas Peter family until it was sold in 1924 to Treve Holman.

Further planting, in particular of rhododendrons including R. 'Cornish Red' was carried out at the end of the 19th century by John Thomas-Peter.

It was not until after 1924, when Treve Holman bought the property, that any real gardening took place. Treve Holman was encouraged by J C Williams in the late 1920s to create a woodland garden in an area beyond the lake. He recommended Hilliers as being a first class nursery and they sent down Harold as a young member of the family on his first ever advisory visit. Harold is now recognised as one of this century's greatest plantsmen and he kept a fatherly eye on the garden until the day he died. Later, in 1937, Bobby Jenkinson of Knapp Hill Nurseries was also employed to create a spectacular arrangement of Japanese azaleas and maples.

Treve Holman subscribed to Frank Kingdon-Ward's expeditions to the Far East when many seeds were brought back to Chyverton to be raised and planted out in the garden.

In addition to the wide selection of Asiatic magnolias and rhododendrons, Treve Holman planted a hedge of *Myrtus luma* in 1948. This is now 6m (20ft) high and is a stunning sight with its beautifully patterned cinnamon coloured bark and tiny white flowers.

After Treve's death in 1959 his son Nigel, fortunately equally interested in the garden, carried on with new plantings. Particularly passionate about magnolias, he introduced many rare and exciting species to the garden. Of particular interest is the very tender *Magnolia macrophylla dealbata* (syn. *M. dealbata*) from Mexico, which has leaves of an astonishing 75cm (30") long and enormous white flowers to match.

Further away from the house is a series of glades, each with its own particular range of connoisseur plants including unusual rhododendrons, azaleas, maples and birches.

Swathes of primulas flourish next to a small stream where the skunk cabbage runs amok, seeding like mustard and cress. Both *Lysichiton camtschatcensis* and *L. americanum* grow here, and they have even produced a natural hybrid with creamy flowers. The moist environment of the stream and its banks also provides ideal conditions for tree ferns, including the especially tender *Cyathea dealbata* with its lovely silver-backed fronds.

Despite a lack of labour, the garden continues to expand into its surrounding woodland, containing a great plant collection framed by John Thomas's magical setting. Although the garden is not open on a regular basis – to do so would mean creating paths which would be out of keeping with the ambience of the garden – the owner is happy to welcome gardeners by appointment.

Location: North of A30, Zelah, near Truro
Tel: (01872) 540 324
Facilities: Toilets, Dogs on leads, Car & Coach Park.

Cotehele, St Dominic

Cotehele nestles into a steep valley on the west bank of the Tamar. The beautiful old house, parts of which are unchanged since the 15th century, is surrounded by a variety of formal and informal gardens.

The earliest map of the estate, dating back to 1550-60, is very simple but shows woodlands, deer park and vestiges of the old medieval strip field system. The earliest written description is by Carew in his survey of Cornwall (1602) – "A mile above Halton standeth Cuttayle, from the French Courtaile, in English short-cut; for the salt water course is here straightened by the encroaching banks. The buildings are ancient, large, strong and fair, and appurtananced with the necessities of wood, water, fishing, parks and mills." "Cotehele" is now thought to be derived from Cornish "Wood on an Estuary".

Not shown on the map, but also dating from an early period are the ancient dovecote and stewponds.

By 1731, Doidge's Map indicated that the present shape of the estate – roads, drives and park – had largely been achieved. However, by this time the Edgcumbe family had to all intents and purposes left Cotehele to concentrate on their estate at Mount Edgcumbe where all their energies (and presumably money!) were spent improving the garden which was to become one of the most famous and well visited gardens of the 17th and 18th centuries.

The house at Cotehele ceased to be used full time by the family and Cotehele escaped any "improvement" until the 1860s when the gardens were laid out. Prior to this in the early 19th century, the gardens were very modest, the main attraction being the magnificent woodlands and in particular the Spanish chestnut trees, one of which was a three-trunked specimen which had an astounding diameter of 11ft 5ins. Unfortunately both this tree and hundreds of others fell in the gales of 1891, when it was estimated that over 100,000 cubic feet of timber was lost.

In 1862 the east front of the house was altered and the three terraces laid out. The area to the north of the house was drained and a formal "Italian" garden created. It was also at this time that the 3rd Earl of Mount Edgcumbe, a great traveller, provided plants for the development of the valley garden.

Although in the early days the house walls were bare and unadorned, the Victorian period saw the introduction of many plants which were used to clothe the ancient stones. These include wisteria and the 'Félicité Perpetué', 'McCartney' and Banksian roses. Also sheltered by the walls are various tender shrubs and climbers, including a fine myrtle and abelia.

The west tower is surrounded by an informal meadow with spring flowers and a number of old trees including an ancient mulberry. The path to the gate leading to the Prospect Tower is edged with eucryphias, medlar and quince.

The upper garden contains a formal lily pond flanked by herbaceous beds containing tender plants such as fuchsia and agapanthus, whilst of particular note is a striking ash tree, *Fraxinus excelsior* 'Jaspidea', known for its golden bark.

Nearby, a nursery garden is used for producing cut flowers for the house.

The south front of the house faces the Bowling Green which is lined with sycamores, the most ancient of which is approximately 150 years old.

The East Terraces are on three levels – the middle and lower terraces have borders of roses under-planted with stachys and aubretia, and two young magnolias have replaced very old examples lost in the 1990 storm. From the terraces the path curves downwards into the lovely valley garden where a thatched Victorian summerhouse overlooks the medieval stewpond and dovecote.

This sheltered valley provides an ideal position for many exotic trees and shrubs. Early rhododendrons and maples are followed by enkianthus, hydrangeas and hoherias whilst at ground level are charming moisture loving plants such as primulas, mimulus and hostas.

From the valley garden the path leads through

The medieval dovecote at Cotehele

into the quiet beauty of the woodlands, from which the river can be seen. Cotehele Wood, an inspiration to artists and travellers down the centuries, retains its sylvan beauty throughout the seasons of the year, with a rich ground flora complemented by a diverse range of tree species.

Location: St Dominick, Saltash
Tel: National Trust (01579) 351 346
Facilities: Disabled Access, Teas, Toilets, Plant Sales, No Dogs, Car & Coach Park. NB Licensed restaurant and small tea room on quay.

Creed, Grampound

Creed House was built in about 1730 and was formerly the Rectory. A mile from the ancient township of Grampound, and set deep in beautiful countryside surrounded by enchanting lanes, meadows and woodlands, it looks down over the granite tower of the 14th Century Church of St. Crida to the River Fal and Golden Valley.

When the present owners took over in 1974 it was a nostalgic forgotten garden, neglected for 50 years. The front lawn was a hayfield and the banks were infested with brambles. The rest of the garden was an impenetrable jungle of laurels and sycamore, festooned with old man's beard, through which could be glimpsed signs of what used to be a fine garden, the tops of *Rhododendron arboreum* some 40 ft. high, a magnolia and some clumps of huge gunnera in a watery corner.

Initial work was with the help of a tractor and silage cutter. One of the great delights of the first spring, after clearing the undergrowth, was the thousands of snowdrops and daffodils that sprang to life, and the large old *Magnolia x soulangeana* that was free to bloom again in unfettered profusion.

Over the next ten years, from 1974-84, the bones of the old garden were slowly uncovered. Around 300 trees were felled, some with root-balls above a man's height. These all had to be knocked out and burnt, the ground levelled and lawns reseeded. A large range of interesting shrubs and rhododendrons, and above all trees, to give colour throughout the year, were planted; many of these are now reaching a respectable size. Since 1984 the owners have refined, upgraded and added to the original plantings.

In front of the house there are two spacious lawns. The first is entirely level and is said to have been at one time both a bowling green and a tennis court. The second lawn slopes down to a pond, well stocked with its own breeding shoals of goldfish (subject to the depredations of herons from the valley below) and to a delightful bog garden. This merges into a woodland which incorporates a path along the boundary giving lovely glimpses of Creed Church and the Golden valley. To the north another lawn, set with a bench to encourage enjoyment of the vista, contains a circular lily pond and a grove of really giant gunnera. Also here are some of the original tree rhododendrons which blew down in the gales of 1979. They have regenerated from the old stumps to form a spectacular dome of colour when in bloom.

Behind the house is the summerhouse, restored in 1977. This was formerly so overgrown that the owners had been in residence for a year before they realised that deep inside the jungle a range of buildings was hidden! Behind the summerhouse is a stream garden and waterfall planted with mimulus, giant kingcup, iris and hosta. To the rear of this was uncovered a lower stable yard with an intriguing design of cobbles and associated walls, which has been planted with alpines and sun-loving plants. Above here is another cobbled stable yard, stables and walled garden planted with herbaceous perennials and still being developed. Wide steps lead to two and a half acres of mixed indigenous trees, planted in 1983. Here rides are kept mown to allow easy access to enjoy the developing woodland.

The Old Rectory garden at Creed

The owners' intention to preserve the serenity of a Rectory garden whilst adding new delights to the plant collection has certainly been realised.

Location: south of A390, Grampound near Truro
Tel: (01872) 530 372
Facilities: Unsuitable for Disabled, Toilets, Dogs on leads. (Teas and plant sales on charity days only)
N.B. Parking of cars in lane by garden.

Enys, Penryn

Enys is first mentioned in 1450 in a Cornish play when it was apparently given as a reward to the builder of the Universe! The gardens were celebrated as early as 1720 in Magna Britannia and late in the 18th century Borlase shows a large formal walled garden with pavilions.

In common with many other Cornish gentry, John Enys and his son Samuel were shrewd enough to marry wealthy heiresses and were therefore able to spend large sums of money on the improvement of both house and garden.

The early garden lay-out remained in place until the beginning of the 19th century when changes began to sweep through the estate. These were initiated by Francis Enys who demolished part of the walled garden and created less formal gardens containing "a delightful shrubbery, with a fresh water lake, a handsome temple, and most delicious walks, shaded with a rich variety of foliage" (Gilbert 1820).

Today, alas, the "handsome temple" is nowhere to be seen, but the gardens remain much the same with their "delicious walks", in particular those next to the ponds, which in spring are a most wonderful sight with myriads of primulas lining the banks.

These ponds were originally quite formal features – known as canals – and were shown on early maps with orchards between them and the house.

Later, however, extensive plantings of the new trees and shrubs, flooding into the country from the 19th-century plant hunters, changed this area completely and at the same time the sides of the ponds were altered to make more sinuous edges.

Towards the end of the 19th century, considerable planting at Enys was carried out as a result of one of the Enys family being himself a keen explorer and plant hunter. During his travels in Patagonia and New Zealand, J D Enys sent home many plants and seeds, including the beautiful Chatham Island Forget-Me-Not (*Myosotidium hortensia*) which was said, in spite of its tender

The lower lake at Enys

nature, to have flourished against a north wall. The fine Chilean laurel (*Laurelia serrata*) that still exists probably dates from this period, as do the roses planted on the arches in the flower garden.

The Cornish cross set amongst a rockery with ferns has been uncovered relatively recently. In Victorian times the rockwork would have been kept bare in order to show off the wide variety of geological specimens – many of them specific to Cornwall and found during mining operations.

The garden was severely damaged by the 1990 gales; clearance works and replanting are still taking place. The garden is normally open for the bluebell season when the drifts of bluebells under the mature trees are one of its glories. The beautiful pools in the valley should not be missed, and there are plenty of choice specimens of rhododendron, azaleas and particularly fine clumps of bamboo, including the rare *Thamnocalamus* situated at the side of the main drive. Also along the drive can be seen some enormous specimens of *Mahonia japonica* 'Bealei'.

The sheltered and enclosed flower garden has an enormous *Actinidia deliciosa* rampaging over the trees and shrubs and, unusually, a specimen of mistletoe growing on a branch of *Acer japonicum*.

Location: St Gluvias, Penryn – south off A39 towards Mylor
Tel: (01326) 373 242

Estray Parc, Budock

Estray Parc was at one time part of Penwarne estate (see below) and its full, rather grandiose, title is The Estray Parc of Hundred Pound in the Bailiwick of Kerrier. This is derived from the fact that its possessors, who were *ipso facto* bailiffs for the Hundred of Kerrier, could impound cattle from all parts of it, i.e. Breage to Mylor and Gwennap to the Lizard. Estray or Estraie is the medieval spelling of the word Stray – the fields behind the house are called the Stray or Estray fields and the one immediately behind them is Pound Field where the animals were impounded if they had not been redeemed within a certain time and the fine paid.

In 1983 the house had a small garden surrounding it, a field on the south-east side and a former orchard and fruit garden on the land on the south-west side, with a stream running between them. The owners, having left Penwarne partly because of the size of the garden, set about creating another garden which now covers about three and a half acres. There were some apple trees, a medlar and a mulberry tree and a huge and spectacular oak tree with a girth of 17 feet. The east side of the stream was re-seeded and planted with laurels, *Rhododendron ponticum* and fast growing conifers along the boundary as a wind break, followed by masses of shrubs as a second hedge. These include camellias, witch hazels, rhododendrons, azaleas camellias, witch hazels, rhododendrons, azaleas and mimosas. The grass on the west side, totally neglected since 1969, is now maintained by frequent cutting and as the shrubs increase in size, the areas of lawn become less. Some of the rhododendrons near the boundary at the bottom were brought back as seed from the Himalayas and have leaves up to 15ins long. There is also a seedling magnolia near the recently re-created ponds which has dark red flowers and is unnamed. Since 1983 many indigenous and specimen trees have been planted on the steep bank known as the Long Hill and, together with groups of typical Cornish shrubs between them and the stream, make a blaze of colour in the spring.

Newer plantings include specimens to give year round colour and texture.

Location: Near Penjerrick, Budock, Falmouth
Tel: (01326) 250 308
Facilities: Unsuitable for Disabled, No Dogs, Car Park.

Falmouth, Fox Rosehill Gardens

These gardens are rather unobtrusively sited between the sea and the main shopping area of the town. However, their rather plain frontage hides many exotic splendours within.

Created as a private garden by the famous Fox family (also of Glendurgan and Trebah), they were started in the 19th century and were to become one of Cornwall's most famous collections of exotic plants.

A French visitor of that period was inspired to write "I was struck by the beauty of his (R W Fox) gardens, which have justly been compared with those of the Hesperides. The orange, date and lemon trees pass the winter here in the open air, grow freely and bear ripe fruit. I saw a tree there from which one hundred and twenty three lemons were plucked in one day, all excellent and much sweeter than those sold in the shops. Mr Fox has naturalized more than three hundred exotic species, he has thus brought together the plants of Australia and New Zealand, the trees of cold and hot countries, loaded all the year round with flowers and fruit."

This astonishing situation continued into the early years of the 20th century, but after the Second World War the gardens were given to the town of Falmouth. The land was split up and Falmouth School of Art developed on part of it. However, much of the original planting remains and the conservatory has recently been renewed with a

Exotics at Fox Rosehill, Falmouth

foreground planting of interesting succulents.

A large vista lined by several Chusan palms (*Trachycarpus fortunei*) is present within the gardens. Other species of palm have been added to the collection including Canary date palm (*Phoenix canariensis*) and Chilean wine palm (*Jubaea chilensis*).

Flowering trees of note include embothrium, davidia, myrtles, liriodendron and tree rhododendrons.

Bamboos are also a feature of the gardens – a particularly stunning sight are the yellow and pink striped culms of *Drepanostachyum hookerianum*.

Other astonishing plants are large specimens of banana (both *Musa basjoo* and *M. ensete*), the Bromeliads – *Fascicularia bicolor* and *pitcairniifolia* and the enormous 20-foot high flower spikes of *Furcraea longaeva*.

There is also a good range of tender aloes, yuccas, etc. in the grounds of the college.

Location: Melvill Road, Falmouth
Tel: Carrick District Council (01872) 224 355
Facilities: Disabled Access, Dogs on leads,
Car & Coach Parking nearby.

Falmouth, Gyllyngdune Gardens

These gardens, a complete contrast to Fox-Rosehill, originated in the mid 19th century when the estate was bought by General Coope. His son, the Rev. William J Coope, laid out the quarry garden in 1837 with its shell grotto, together with tunnels under the lane for access to beach and changing rooms. The small folly known as Parson Coope's Chapel, which probably functioned as a summerhouse overlooking the sea, was also built at this time, together with the *faux* "Stonehenge" feature on the cliff.

The 'Stonehenge' feature at Gyllyngdune Gardens, Falmouth

After being owned by the Waters and Horniman families from 1863 onwards, it was bought by the town council in 1903 who decided to turn it into a public park to accommodate the increasing number of tourists. A bandstand was built together with the Princess Pavilion and its verandah. These typically late Victorian features can still be seen, and form the focal point for bedding plants which vary with the season. Dating from the original planting is an enormous *Brugmansia suaveolens* with its fragrant trumpets. The charming bandstand is matched by the lovely and immensely heavy iron seats underneath the verandah, which, interestingly, were retrieved from the decks of a Royal Mail steamer.

Location: Princess Pavilion, Melville Road, Falmouth
Tel: Carrick District Council (01872) 224 355
Facilities: Part Disabled Access, Teas, Toilets, Dogs on leads, Car Park.

Falmouth, Queen Mary Gardens

These gardens, on the site of former marshes, were specifically constructed for the enjoyment of the seaside visitors who were arriving in vast numbers by the beginning of the 20th century. They have always been laid out with summer bedding and this practice has been continued with the added recent bonus of renovation to include a 300ft long herbaceous border and tropical bedding.

Location: Cliff Road, Falmouth
Tel: Carrick District Council (01872) 224 355
Facilities: Disabled Access, Toilets, Dogs on leads, Car & Coach Park nearby.

Furzeball Cottage, Lanteglos-by-Fowey

Although it is difficult to establish the size of the original settlement, from Elizabethan times onwards there were two cottages on the site known in the 18th century as Forsters Cottages. The gardens were small, measured at 1 rod and 9 perches, with Furzeball Hill and waste extending to 2 acres. Later maps of the 19th century show one cottage with the name of Firswall, a tied farm labourer's dwelling of two up and two down.

The length of human occupation is demonstrated by the original garden, which over the centuries produced food for many families and their waste helped with its fertility! This accumulation of waste consequently increased the height of the garden above the surrounding fields to a maximum of some eight feet at the lower end behind the summerhouse, so that steps had to be constructed to connect this area with the extended grounds to the north.

In 1954 Joan Gillies, the wife of a New Zealand playwright, bought the property from the Boconnoc estate and planted cottage garden flower beds. A more comprehensive development of the garden followed when Frederic Winter bought the cottage in 1961 and for nearly two decades planted numbers of exotic trees together with numerous varieties of rhododendron and azalea. Pocket gardens were created by the use of hedging and walls and the spring heads were purchased and incorporated into the garden. Following this initial activity was a period of declining maintenance with parts of the garden becoming derelict and overgrown.

In 1985 when Phyllis and Eric Kay purchased Furzeball, they immediately saw the challenge and potential beauty of its garden. Since then they have extended the grounds still further, built steps and constructed footpaths, refurbished the well and springs, dug out the pond and planted new flower beds. The "pocket garden" concept has been continued. This allows the development of discrete areas of cottage garden flower beds, wild flower conservation plots, ornamental shrubs, water and bog gardens. An old greenhouse foundation has been turned into a terrace garden overlooking the tree-lined boundary of silver birch, weeping willow, ash, bird cherry, black poplar and Mediterranean maple. On the northern side, a screen of rhododendrons is punctuated by a magnolia and a tulip tree (*Liriodendron tulipifera*).

Despite its small size (just under 1 acre) the layout gives the feeling of a much larger garden and in winter and spring the flowering shrubs give off a heady scent on sunny days.

Location: Pont, Lanteglos-by-Fowey, Fowey
Tel: (01726) 870 600
Facilities: Part Disabled Access, Dogs on leads, Toilets, Car Park. No Coaches.

Garvinack Woodland Garden, Tregavethan

Garvinack Woodland Garden lies at the very head of the Kenwyn Valley and extends in all to some 25 acres. The river rises in the marshy ground at the north end of the wood, close to the A30, and is fed by several springs. The garden is sheltered from northerly and easterly winds and the woodland has in all probability existed in its present shape and size for well over 200 years. The natural cover is made up of Turkey oaks, beech, ash, holly, hazel, alder, laurel and sycamore. At various times for practical purposes larch, pine and fir have been added. The ground slopes to the south-west and is well drained.

Prior to 1981 the woods and farm were owned for several generations by the Walters family, and it was George Walters who some 30 years ago

indulged his hobby and imagination by underplanting the woodland with camellias, rhododendrons, magnolias and azaleas, of which there are many fine examples and varieties. These are mainly concentrated around the house and at the southern end of the wood where there are some four and a half acres containing well established trees and shrubs.

In the wood is an avenue 60 metres long of over 70 named varieties of camellia. The rhododendron collection is a fine one, and although largely unnamed, includes *hippophaëoides*, *R. schlippenbachii*, *R. macabeanum*, *R. sinogrande* and a fine *R. roxieanum* with its rust coloured indumentum. There are 18 mature magnolia trees, some over 30 ft high and included in this collection are *Magnolia x soulangeana* 'Brozzonii', *M. heptapeta*, *M. dawsoniana*, *M. kobus* and *M. sargentiana* var. *robusta*. The star of this collection is the related *Michelia doltsopa* with its beautiful furry buds and exquisitely scented white flowers.

The present owner is pursuing a policy of reducing the laurels which have tended to dominate, thus giving more light and space to the other flora, whilst maintaining as much as possible of the natural and informal aspect of the wood.

Location: Garvinack Farm, Tregavethan, Truro – south of A30
Tel: (01872) 560 385
Facilities: Part Disabled Access, Teas, Toilets, Plant Sales, Dogs on leads, Car Park nearby.

Glendurgan, Mawnan Smith

Before the arrival of the Fox family, the valley at Durgan was simply an overgrown and marshy area with some surrounding orchards. The Foxes, having already established their Falmouth gardens, decided in the 1820s to create a second home and garden on the site. By 1826 a thatched cottage had been built and the shelter belts of beech, sycamore, oak and conifers had been planted by Alfred Fox and his wife Sarah. After setting out the bones of the garden, they then had time to deal with more exciting projects including planting a laurel maze, (inspired by the one at Sydney Gardens in Bath) and digging a large pond. The wonderful Tulip trees (*Liriodendron tulipifera*) with their gnarled and knotty trunks also date from this period.

At the end of the nineteenth century, George Fox inherited the estate and set about introducing many more trees and shrubs into the garden. Not only did he plant most of the conifers – cedars, cypresses, pines and spruces, he was equally keen on the fragrant rhododendrons and the tender hybrids raised by his relations at Penjerrick. He was also passionate about fruit growing, building up an extensive collection of apples and pears in addition to the more exotic peaches, nectarines and citrus.

After George Henry Fox died in 1931, the garden continued to be the recipient of many treasures. His descendant, Cuthbert Lloyd Fox and his wife, who were equally enthusiastic gardeners, increased the range of plants to include magnolias, cornus, Asiatic rhododendrons and eucryphias.

The Bog Garden at Glendurgan

Plan of the Maze at Sydney Gardens, Bath – the model for Glendurgan

Realizing that the spaces in a garden are as important as the plantings, they resisted the temptation to cram plants into every available nook and cranny. The results of this restraint are the lovely glades scattered with wild flowers and the mossy banks studded with primroses and ferns.

The National Trust, since taking over the garden in 1962, has endeavoured to maintain these beautiful spaces whilst at the same time carrying out necessary work on plants which are the victims of maturity and old age. The maze needed drastic action and in 1979 underwent hard pruning, feeding and under-drainage. Between 1992 and 1994 it underwent a complete restoration to its original plan.

The small valley to the west had become overgrown. Clearance of this area has allowed room for delicate plantings of marsh lovers and later in the year, hydrangeas with their soft blues and whites.

Recent plantings include new and tender conifers, which only survive in the mildest areas of Britain. Another recent project has been the recon-struction of the summerhouse at the centre of the maze in its original Victorian style.

Location: Mawnan Smith near Falmouth
Tel: National Trust (01326) 250 906
Facilities: Tea House, Plant Sales, Toilets, No Dogs, Car & Coach Park.

Godolphin, Helston

Godolphin was first shown on a map of the County of Cornwall in 1576, but the first recorded mention of the garden was in 1690 by Francis Godolphin writing to his godfather, John Evelyn (of "Sylva" fame) –

"it stands on the side of a hill and is a very good seat... 'tis a large old house built, the front upon pillars with flat arches both within and without... an abundance of trees about it and a great deal of the garden not walled but fenced with Hedges."

The Goldophins, whose mine was located nearby, were extremely wealthy and influential during the 16th and 17th centuries; but after the family left the house for fame and fortune in London, the house and gardens were forgotten and untouched by fashion during subsequent centuries.

The house lies on the north side of Godolphin Hill surrounded by gardens and farm enclosures. The hill was at one time partially emparked for a deer park and recent research has shown that an area known as the "Slips" could perhaps have been connected with the park and used for running deer through for sporting purposes.

The Side and Pond Gardens are even more fascinating and are shown on an estate map of 1786, laid out as nine formal plots planted round with hedges, with a central walk and two stewponds to the south-west of the garden.

The Stew Pond at Godolphin in winter – Painting by Elmer Schofield

Stylistically the gardens could be of any age from Tudor to the early 1700s but it is probable that they date from the early 17th century when the house was re-modelled by Sir Francis Godolphin I. Within the nine compartments, complicated knot patterns would have been set out, to be viewed from the raised walks.

In addition, there were groves and avenues of trees amongst which were wooden statues, which were believed to have existed up until the end of the 19th century but have now disappeared. Today, the area to the south of the house is intriguingly full of bumps and hollows that were probably part of the greater landscape.

Although a great deal of work remains to be done at Godolphin, restoration work is under way with the owners keen to create a garden in context with the history of the house.

No Elizabethan garden of this size has been brought back to life before. This exciting project aims to re-capture some of that great Elizabethan garden ambience.

Location: Godolphin Cross, Breage, Helston, off the B3302
Tel: (01736) 762 409

Grignan, Penwartha, Perranporth

Located in the sheltered Penwartha Coombe valley near the hamlet of Bolingey, this garden has been developed by Mr and Mrs Ted Penna over the last 40 years from a green field site. The stream and leat which swirl and sparkle through the garden have been used to good effect; with a series of precarious planks across the water to give added excitement! Lovely golden candelabra primulas grow in the shade amidst wonderful clumps of Royal fern. Nearer to the house the beds of delphiniums and lupins give a cottage atmosphere; whilst in contrast, a weeping beech is set against a white wall with yellow and red plantings. The stumps of old apple trees have roses and clematis growing up them and the surrounding fences are also well clad.

A short walk away is a nature reserve set in a hillside woodland which has many of the indicator species associated with ancient woods – bluebells, wood anemones and dog's mercury. Walking sticks are thoughtfully provided to assist the less agile around the walk.

Location: Penwartha, Perranporth, 400 yards from Bolingey Inn.
Tel: (01872) 573 382
Facilities: Light Teas, Plant Sales, No Dogs, Car Park. It is preferable to telephone for an appointment.

Hall Walk, Fowey

Although not strictly a garden, Hall Walk is of interest in view of its survival from the Elizabethan period.

At that time, walks were a feature of many grand gardens; another remnant example is to be found at St Winnow where the public footpath still runs through the Barton Walk orchard.

Here at Hall, the walk has been in use for four hundred years, having been created by the Mohuns of Hall in the 16th century. Charles I visited the walk in the following century, not just to admire the view, but also to inspect its strategic importance. It was here that he narrowly escaped assassination – just after he passed a shot rang out across the river, killing a fisherman at the rear of the royal party.

Carew's detailed description of the walk as he found it in 1600 is as follows:-

"[The walk is] cut out in the side of a steep hill whose foot the salt water washeth, evenly levelled to serve for bowling, floored with sand for soaking up the rain, closed with two shorn hedges, and banked with sweet scenting flowers. It wideneth to a sufficient breadth for the march of five or six in front,

and extendeth to not much less than half a London mile; neither doth it lead wearisomely forthright, but yieldeth varied and yet not overbusy turnings as the ground's opportunity affordeth, which advantage increaseth the prospect, and is converted on the foreside into platforms for the planting of ordnance and the walkers' sitting, and on the back part into summer-houses for their more private retreat and recreation..."

Today one can still see a number of holly trees (which were presumably at one time the "shorn hedges") and a shelter, which is ideally situated at the end of the walk as a resting place for the weary!

Although Fowey has lost its strategic importance, the walk has lost none of its spectacular view, and now belongs to the National Trust, having been given by Colonel Shakerley in 1945 to commemorate the men of Lanteglos and Fowey who were lost in the Second World War. A granite memorial records this event, and a further monument to the great Cornish writer Sir Arthur Quiller-Couch can also be found above Penleath Point.

Location: Bodinnick, near Fowey

Headland, Polruan-by-Fowey

The house at Headland, Polruan, perches on a levelled shelf of the cliff overlooking the River Fowey, in what was once a village quarry. The river is on one side and the sea on the other, with a magical view of Dodman Point and the Lizard beyond.

Hebes and Mesembryanthemums at Headland Garden

The garden was started when the house was built in 1921 and its creation must have required large quantities of topsoil to fill the otherwise barren crevices between the rocks. Although it became well known enough to be occasionally open to the public, by 1974 when the Hills took over, it was quite overgrown.

Although the basic structure of the garden was in place, many more terraces and interconnecting paths have been built. Local pebbles and rocks from the beach have been hauled up to reinforce walls and rock faces. This use of natural stone has been most effective – the natural rock faces merge imperceptibly into walls pierced with arches, and ledges evolve into seats.

The vegetable garden lies at the top of a vertical drop into a tiny cove below. In spite of this, good crops of fruit and vegetable are gathered, the fertility of the soil having been improved by liberal applications of seaweed.

A number of large pines from the original plantings are reaching the end of their lives and also have the added complication of shallow soil which gives little support to the rooting system. Two huge specimens of Monterey cypress (*Cupressus macrocarpa*) have blown down, one right over the cliff, creating quite a disposal problem. The top was sawn up and carried from the beach in pieces whilst the stump was towed away by the Harbour Authorities! Wind is, of course, a perpetual problem – when the pines are too much buffeted by gales, the needles are damaged, consequently whole branches die and have to be taken off. However, many seedlings have been planted to provide for the next generation. Both these and newly planted shrubs are surrounded with a mesh cylinder to filter wind for the first winter.

Successful deciduous trees are hawthorn, mountain ash and purple beech which, although growing in a distorted manner and remaining quite stunted, provide an attractive contrast to the evergreens.

Hedging species such as escallonia, *Hippophaë rhamnoïdes* and euonymus are also successful, the hedges having been shaped to the lines of the cliff to reduce wind damage.

Although many types of hebe have been tried, it is the old original plantings that have survived, seeding into crevices and providing offspring for replanting.

A real success is pampas grass which has been planted at the edge of a sheer drop on the south-west boundary. It serves two purposes – firstly, it holds the rocky overhangs together and reduces erosion; and secondly, it deters children from climbing over the boundary wall to oblivion!

Although frosts are infrequent, the lashing winter gales arrive with unremitting regularity.

Plants are not only battered and broken, but sometimes are blown right out of the ground. It is the frost laden south-easterly winds that do the most damage to the succulents that are a particular feature of the garden. These succulents provide a feast of colour in the summer with lampranthus and Hottentot fig (*Carpobrotus edulis*) smothering the rocks. Another successful succulent is *Aptenia cordifolia* with its bright green fleshy leaves and red rosettes making a wonderful ground cover.

In addition to these exotics, the rocks are festooned with many different lichens whose beautiful textures and subtle colours give added dimension and contrast.

Location: 3 Battery Lane, Polruan-by-Fowey
Tel: (01726) 870 243
Facilities: Teas, Toilets, No Dogs.
N.B. Disabled welcome but very difficult for wheelchairs, crutches possible.

The Lost Gardens of Heligan, Mevagissey

When the gardens of Heligan began to reveal their secrets to the restoration team in 1991, no-one could have imagined the impact of their discovery and subsequent re-awakening upon the public imagination. Almost overnight, the extraordinary energy of the volunteers and professionals, combined with generous public, private and corporate sponsorship, established Heligan as the largest garden restoration in Europe. Heligan's fame, however, is not due to having been laid out by a "Repton" or a "Capability Brown" – but more visitors now come here than to any other private garden in the country. Heligan's importance and romance lie in the fact that it was all but forgotten for so long, and its subsequent restoration gives us a window onto the working life of an extraordinary garden.

The estate dates from the early 17th century, when a branch of the Tremayne family moved here from Devon. They remained for the next three hundred years until the outbreak of the First World War, when the house was used as a convalescent home for officers. Most of the twenty-two garden staff went off to fight, many of them never to return. The Tremaynes came back for a while after the war but their hearts were no longer here and the gardens slowly went to sleep, although a succession of tenants tried to keep the main walks open. Today nearly seventy acres of pleasure grounds contain a magnificent plant collection together with a range of exotic glasshouses, working buildings, romantic structures and

The Flower Garden at Heligan

designed landscapes, reflecting the past passions and interests of the family. The combination of these and the mild Cornish climate has conspired to create a garden, or in truth a series of gardens within a garden, which are unique.

The pleasure gardens contain rare and beautiful shrubs, including the exquisite "Hooker" collection of original Himalayan rhododendrons and other exotics collected from around the world by the intrepid plant hunters of the last century; they also provide the backcloth to numerous romantic structures such as the Northern Summerhouse with its sea views and cobbled floor, the Fern Ravine, the Italian Garden, the Crystal Grotto (whose candlelit interior was used as a romantic backdrop on summer evenings) and the Wishing Well.

Through a mass of luxuriant vegetation in New Zealand one can glimpse the mysterious arched recesses of one of the finest Beebole walls in the country. The latest project, begun in 1995, is the walled Sundial Garden, described one hundred years ago in the *Gardeners' Chronicle* as containing "the finest herbaceous border in England".

The Productive Gardens at Heligan are perhaps most famous for being a "living museum" of 19th-century horticulture. The celebration of the skills of the ordinary men and women who made gardens such as these great, has been sadly neglected elsewhere. It is here that the Head Gardener reigned supreme, growing all the fruit, vegetables, herbs, ornamental flowers and exotics for the Big House. The heart of his kingdom comprised four walled gardens with associated pits, frames, glasshouses and working buildings, a large kitchen garden and various orchards; the restoration of which is now nearly complete.

More than 300 varieties of fruit and vegetable are being grown again by traditional methods. In the Melon Garden one can marvel at the ingenuity of the country's only remaining manure-heated pineapple pits; whilst in the great walled Flower Garden, alongside the glasshouses for citrus, vine and peach, is the most comprehensive collection of Victorian cut flowers in the country. There are also working buildings – the boiler houses, tool and potting sheds, equipment store, fruit store, dark house and bothies.

The main view from the "Big House" (not open to the public) was down "The Jungle" valley to the picturesque fishing village of Mevagissey. It was created at the time when a new passion for sub-tropical plants swept the country one hundred and fifty years ago. Only in the frost-free valleys of Cornwall could this passion fulfil its promise, and "The Jungle" is a breathtaking example of its kind. The steep-sided valley contains four ponds one above the other, nestling in lush vegetation, and is

home to a large collection of tree ferns, palms, bamboos and exotic specimen trees.

Work has started on the recently discovered 27-acre "Lost Valley", thought to be part of an English "Picturesque" landscape. *The Times* described Heligan as "the garden restoration of the century" – it is certainly a unique opportunity to see work in progress and history in the making.

Location: Pentewan near St Austell; take Gorran Haven turning off the B3273.
Tel: (01726) 844 157
Facilities: Part Disabled Access, Tearoom, Picnic Area, Toilets, Plant Sales, Dogs on leads, Car & Coach Park.

Higher Truscott, Launceston

Higher Truscott is situated at the edge of the hamlet of Truscott at 550 feet above sea level on a gentle south facing slope. Although the elevation has the advantage of good frost drainage, it is exposed to winds from all directions with cold easterlies frequently causing damage.

The garden is in two parts. The first, started in 1962, complements the old long house and farm buildings and is intended as a view from the house giving variation in form and texture as well as colour at all times of the year.

The soil has a neutral pH which allows a wide variety of subjects to be grown. It is also shallow and stony so that drainage is no problem, but plants requiring moisture during the growing season are at risk, especially in a dry summer. Incorporation of large quantities of organic matter and heavy mulches has been necessary to conserve moisture and maintain fertility.

Many trees and shrubs have been planted to provide both shelter and shade and are accompanied by dense under-planting. Camellias, magnolias and rhododendrons provide the main spring colour with smaller subjects, especially naturalized fritillaries and hybrid hellebores, giving varied interest.

The problem of alternate wet and dry conditions has been stressful to plants, this together with wind-rock predisposes them to infection with honey fungus which claims victims annually. The other major curse is slugs, owing to the large quantity of dead organic material. The combination of slugs and wind make it impossible to grow plants such as delphiniums and lupins. However, the owners take a positive view in that at least the casualties give an opportunity for new planting!

The second part of the garden, across the lane, was started in 1980 and is even more exposed, but has as a backdrop a splendid view of Launceston Castle with Dartmoor on the horizon. Here the

The rock garden at Higher Truscott

planting is mixed but predominantly herbaceous for summer colour.

The theme is informality using island beds cut into the old pony paddock which gradually blend into the countryside. This leads down to a fruit and vegetable garden with formal features of box and herbs with a summerhouse and vegetables grown in raised "no-dig" beds.

The growing of alpines on rocky outcrops has met with mixed success because of the climate; more successful have been the troughs planted with tiny treasures and a small greenhouse which has been adapted as an alpine house. A bulb frame allows bulbous subjects requiring a summer baking to be grown, which is quite impossible in the open ground.

The owners have a particular interest in climbers, especially clematis, and plants which have been selected for their permanent nature and ability to provide interest all year round.

Location: St Stephens near Launceston – left of A388
Tel: (01566) 772 755
Facilities: Part Disabled Access, Teas, Toilets, Plant Sales, No Dogs, Car Park.
N.B. Guide Dogs permitted. Coach parking by appointment only.

The Hollies, Grampound

This garden of about 2 acres lies unexpectedly behind an old cottage fronting onto the main St Austell-Truro road, and is an old site dating back hundreds of years. The family started "gardening" here in the early 1700s and the following generations have carried on.

The garden, a long thin plot, opens onto an old orchard and three fields, part of a medieval lay-out known as a "Stitch". The principal philosophy is to have something interesting or unusual all the year round, based on a Cottage Garden theme.

Steps from the back of the house lead up past many old granite troughs of all sizes full of alpines to a lawn area surrounded by herbaceous borders. A small gate leads from the end of the lawn to a small space containing shade-loving plants and a tiny pond. A grass walk full of snowdrops, crocus, fritillaries and cyclamen leads to the vegetable patch. On the way down, another gate opens into the Plantation. This is the old orchard and is planted with island beds of trees, shrubs and herbaceous plants. In keeping with the natural and informal style of the garden a "kissing gate" leads into the fields, thus merging the cultivated with the natural areas beyond.

Location: Grampound near Truro

One of the garden compartments at The Hollies

Tel: (01726) 882 474
Facilities: Disabled Access, Teas, Toilets, Plant Sales, No
Dogs, Car & Coach Park nearby.

Ince Castle

Ince Castle Gardens, Saltash

Ince Castle was built in the 1640s of small pink
bricks, probably from the Netherlands, on a
promontory jutting out into the St Germans or
Lynher River near Plymouth. Although not
regarded as a real castle by military historians, the
walls are over three feet thick and the roof parapet
is castellated.

From the garden there are extensive views down
the river to the Tamar, across to the park of Antony
House (from which many of the shrubs at Ince
came) and up to Sheviock Wood near St Germans.

Patricia Viscountess Boyd, with her late
husband, bought Ince in 1960 and created the
present large garden. In 1994 she gave the house to
her son and daughter-in-law who now live there
with her.

In spring the main interest comes from the
shrubs in the wood, mostly arranged round a
clearing described in an 1805 drawing as a Bowling
Green. To the south of the house is a formal garden
containing plants of interest from April to the
autumn. Here there is a Shell House filled with
shells collected from British colonies by the late
Lord Boyd. The adjacent spinney, composed
mostly of lime trees, is a mass of daffodils and

narcissus in March and April, followed swiftly by a
sea of wild chervil. In early summer the little white
garden is at its best, while the walled garden has
plants which continue to the end of the summer.

Since moving to the house in 1994 the present
Lord Boyd and his wife have flattened the lawn to
the east of the house to improve the view of the
river from the ground floor rooms, and placed at
the entrance to the forecourt beside the enormous
fallen Turkey oak, the stone lions which were made
to go on Admiralty Arch at the end of the Mall in
London. They also built the conservatory.

Location: Saltash. At Stoketon Cross on A38 west of
Saltash, Trematon and Elmgate signpost.
Tel: (01752) 842672

Ken-Caro, near Liskeard

Planting was initiated at Ken-Caro in 1970, with a
further major extension in 1993. A thoughtfully
designed and well labelled garden, it is noted for its
fine range of plants set off to perfection by the
wonderful views of the rolling hills of Dartmoor in
the distance.

Structural planting is provided by a variety of
conifers including *Chamaecyparis lawsoniana*
'Kilmacurragh', *C.l.* 'Buckland Gold' and *C.l.*
Smithii.

The soil is very acid and all the usual acid-loving

Ken-Caro

species grow well here, aided by copious amounts of farmyard manure to help retain moisture and give added fertility.

In addition to the spring interest of rhododendrons, camellias and a diversity of pieris, seasonal colour has been extended by extensive plantings of abutilon, eucryphia and hydrangea together with many variegated plants for year-round interest and a wide selection of herbaceous perennials.

Amongst the more unusual plants in the garden is a *Lomatia ferruginea*, now about 12 years old and 16 feet high – a handsome evergreen shrub, it has scarlet and yellow flowers in summer, and flourishes in spite of its tender reputation.

Location: Bicton, near Liskeard – north of A390
Tel: (01579) 362 446
Facilities: Plant Sales, No Dogs, Car & Coach Park.

Lamorran House, St Mawes

Lying at the tip of the Roseland peninsula overlooking the sea, this exciting garden has been developed, largely since 1982, by Robert Dudley-Cooke, taking its inspiration from the gardens of the Mediterranean region.

The garden, of approximately four acres, is situated on a steep south-facing slope with a congenial microclimate. Shelter from sea winds has been of paramount importance, and is provided both by existing trees and new planting of various types of pine and eucalyptus in those areas where expansion of the garden has taken place.

The aim of the owner has been to create an intimate multi-level garden with year-round interest with particular emphasis on sub-tropical plants and larger rhododendrons and azaleas.

Initial work involved the moving of a large collection of rhododendrons and azaleas from the owner's former garden in Surrey. A Japanese garden was created with over 1000 examples of evergreen azaleas flowering from the end of January through into July. Harmonization of the various colour forms has been particularly important with gradual changes between colours together with plenty of white to offset the bolder colours. Visitors will be surprised to see many of the so-called indoor azaleas flowering happily in the garden. Many tender rhododendrons are also to be found here including 'Countess of Haddington' and 'White Wings'. The Japanese garden is not merely a collection of plants but also features a pretty pond with its source in a small grotto. Further streams and ponds are to be found with a diversity of planting themes throughout the garden.

The Mediterranean area of the garden features

Ochagavia sp. (Bromeliaeceae) at Lamorran

not only water but also an arresting rock face topped by a small classical style gazebo. In the lower garden is a classical bridge from which visitors can find an uninterrupted view over to the lighthouse on St Antony's and beyond. The bridge crosses a small rocky stream backed by a bank of succulents dominated by large agaves, aloes, puyas and under-planted with lampranthus. In this warmer area are to be found tender treasures including acacias, callistemons and grevilleas with lower growing plants such as osteospermums, argyranthemums and arctotis giving stunning summer colour to the banks.

Succulents and palms are also a feature of the garden with the introduction of a number of large specimen plants, particularly palms from Italy, to provide a substantial framework. There are some 15 species represented, complemented by the tree ferns and yucca collection of which *Yucca aloifolia* 'Variegata' makes a particularly arresting display.

Expansion of the garden continues and the visitor can look forward to the implementation of new features which will compliment and contrast with the existing.

Location: Upper Castle Road, St Mawes
Tel: (01326) 270 800
Facilities: Unsuitable for Disabled. Toilets, Plant Sales, No Dogs. Car Parking in road.

The rock face at Lamorran

Lancarffe, Bodmin

There has been a dwelling at Lancarffe at least since the 17th century, but the garden elements that now exist date mainly from the 20th century with some remnants from earlier periods. Many fine old trees are to be seen, including two outstanding Turkey oaks (*Quercus cerris*) and many ancient beeches (*Fagus sylvatica*) which were planted by the Hext family in the early 19th century.

In 1938 the property was purchased by Admiral Sir Bernard Rawlings, who came to live permanently at the house in 1947. When he arrived only a small lawn and vegetable patch existed, and with the help of Lady Rawlings and their family he set about creating a garden almost from scratch; from these basics he was to construct stone terracing and walls which rose from newly seeded lawns; and windbreaks, most necessary on the edge of Bodmin Moor, were also planted. Azalea and acer seeds brought back from Japan were successfully germinated and many of these are still to be seen at Lancarffe, particularly in the area of the drive leading to the house.

In 1956 Philip Gilbert purchased Lancarffe. He and his wife were also keen gardeners and wished to enlarge the garden from its existing one and a half acres. Lawns were extended and further windbreaks planted. At the same time the walled ornamental garden and the round pond were built. Additional acers were planted, together with hybrid and species rhododendrons, magnolias, azaleas, cornus, camellias, hydrangeas and many other shrubs and trees. Today wide mossy paths meander through this area where the maturing hardwoods are under-planted with shrubs.

In the walled kitchen garden a greenhouse is used mainly for growing auriculas, which provide a splendid splash of colour, and another greenhouse contains two vines, a *Lapageria rosea* and acacias.

Between the windbreaks there are fine views to the west and north. The garden has matured beautifully into five acres of formal and informal spaces full of pleasant visual surprises round every corner.

Although Philip Gilbert died in 1970, his son Richard and family take a keen interest in the garden and are adding continuously to the stock. They are ably assisted by the gardener Mr William Andrews, who has been here for 35 years.

Amongst the many rare and interesting plants to be seen are *Paulownia tomentosa*, *Magnolia thompsoniana*, *M. nitida* and *M. rostrata; Telopea truncata*, *Liriodendron tulipifera*, *Camellia* 'White Nun'; *Rhododendron wardii astrocalyx* and a tall *R. baileyi*.

Location: north east of of Bodmin, Off A30
Facilities: Part Disabled Access, Teas, Toilets, Dogs on leads, Car Park.
NB No coach park.

The terraces at Lancarffe

Lanhydrock, Bodmin

Lanhydrock overlooks the River Fowey and is largely a 19th-century landscape overlaying and extending a 17th-century core.

The Robartes family, who bought the estate in 1620, started by planting a great avenue of sycamore in 1648, then ten years later laid out the deer park to the south of the avenue. (The latter survived until the end of the 18th century.)

Nearer to the house stood the charming gatehouse (still existing) which was at the entrance to a walled court in front of the house. An interesting late 17th-century bird's-eye sketch of the house shows this gatehouse together with three walled areas which are simply laid out, one with fruit trees and quartered into four grass plots. Further north, beyond the formal bowling green, an orchard merged with an informal area known as the "wilderness".

By the late 18th century the fashion in garden design had changed, and the formal gardens and walls were removed allowing the parkland to sweep right up to the house.

By 1857 however, the wheel of fashion had turned full circle and Sir George Gilbert Scott, the famous Victorian architect, was employed to design formal gardens around the house. These he laid out on the site of the old gardens, surrounding them with a new castellated wall with decoration to match the gatehouse. Formal planting took place consisting of Irish yews (*Taxus baccata* 'Fastigiata') with elaborate parterres of bedding.

A number of fine late 17th-century bronze urns (originating in the Chateau de Bagatelle) were also placed in this area to provide focal points to the beds.

The main front with yews and rose beds at Lanhydrock

The Higher Garden behind the house was first laid out as a shrub garden in 1860 but was extensively altered about 1933 and most of what is visible today dates from the latter period. This area contrasts with the formal gardens below, and from it excellent views are obtained over the park.

The 7th Viscount Clifden was responsible for the planting of the wonderful mature magnolias in this area. The National Trust, under the auspices of the knowledgeable head gardener Peter Borlase, has added to these over the years, resulting in a renowned collection. The splendid specimens of *Magnolia grandiflora* on the wall of the house represent some of the first plantings of magnolia at Lanhydrock – and must be well into their second century of growth. The garden now holds some 200 magnolias of approximately 120 different species, hybrids and cultivars. Varieties originated at the garden include *M. sprengeri* 'Lanhydrock' and *M. campbellii ssp. mollicomata* 'Peter Borlase'.

Under the large magnolias flows Borlase's Stream, providing a moist spot for hosts of bog plants, including primulas, rodgersias and arums. Beyond lies the yew-hedged circle filled with herbaceous plants flowering in the late summer, the southern half laid out before the First World War, the northern section by the Trust in 1971. The pretty thatched cottage above the circle was occupied in the 19th century but now acts as a summerhouse.

The wooded upper slopes encircling the house are not only planted with the usual Cornish mixture of rhododendron and camellias, but have year-round interest with summer flowering trees and shrubs such as cornus and hydrangea. Many trees have the added dimension of beautiful bark – these include the birches *Betula costata* and *Betula papyrifera*.

Last, but not least, Lanhydrock still has its lovely avenue. Over the years most of the original sycamores have gone, but a few venerable specimens still survive. The majority is now of beech, and these form a double row rather than a single one as originally planned.

Location: Off B3269 near Bodmin
Tel: National Trust (01208) 73320
Facilities: Disabled Access, Teas, Toilets, Plant Sales, No Dogs (except park & woodland), Car & Coach Park. N.B. Restaurant facilities.

Lanterns, Mylor

Tucked into a tiny valley on the south side of Restronguet Creek, the garden at Lanterns is a treasure trove of unusual plants. Work started in 1966 but the majority dates from 1973 when the owners, Mr and Mrs Chapman, retired and started landscaping and planting in earnest. A series of interconnecting paths and steps make the garden appear larger than it really is and there is always something to see in the layered planting structure that has developed over the years.

Larger trees such as eucalyptus and trachycarpus palms shelter the large leaved rhododendrons, the Japanese maples and the tender mimosas. Many and varied climbers scramble through the trees and are also to be found on every available piece of wall.

The ground, too, has an exuberant mixture of herbaceous perennials, bulbs, grasses and ferns. The latter grow particularly well adjacent to the tiny streams that trickle through the garden. Astilbes, arums and irises are also to be found in these wetter areas, together with such fascinating plants as *Arisarum proboscideum*, colloquially known as the Mouse Plant due to its flowers resembling so many mice tails disappearing into the undergrowth.

Amongst more stately plants are *Melianthus major*, the hedychiums and *Euphorbia mellifera*. The luxuriant growth of these and the rest of the astonishing range of plants, both large and small, results in a garden packed full and overflowing with a profusion of plants throughout the year.

The owner grows many named varieties of pelargoniums, some with scented leaves, as well as named fuchsias and hellebores of various sizes and colours, all of which are for sale in season.

Location: Restroguet, Mylor near Falmouth
Tel: (01326) 372 007
Facilities: Picnic Area, Toilets, Plant Sales, Dogs on leads, Limited Car Parking.

Longcross Victorian Garden, Port Isaac

The gardens were laid out in approximately their current form in late Victorian and early Edwardian times. The owner at that time was a Captain Allerdyce who designed the gardens with the help of several local gardeners. After decades of neglect, the process of re-establishing the garden began about 15 years ago and happily the gardens are now back to their former splendour.

The gardens were constructed primarily to overcome the difficulties of the local climate; north Cornwall is England's windiest area with strong winds laden with salt even in the summer. This results in the garden receiving one hundredweight of salt per acre per year! The majority of shrubs in

The fountain at Longcross Garden

the garden have shiny or leathery leaves that afford protection from the salt. These salt tolerant shrubs are positioned in hedge form to protect the garden – this is so effective that even in a gale, areas of the garden can be found which are totally calm.

Entering the gardens, you will notice the tall pine trees, these are Monterey pines (*Pinus radiata*) the survivors of a much larger plantation established in the early days of the garden. The Monterey pine is one of the few trees that can grow to a great height in north Cornwall. Unfortunately they only live for about 100 years and are now dying of old age. In contrast the deciduous trees in the garden are healthy where they receive protection from the hedging but are dead or stunted once a certain height is reached as a result of the salt winds.

The shrubs in the garden represent the range of plants that can tolerate a marine climate which on the positive side has very few frosts or snowfalls. Many shrubs are hardy but not fully hardy, and will not thrive in colder areas. Following excavation of the pathways and borders, several original border plants re-established themselves, notably Welsh poppies, aquilegias and feverfew, and are now semi-naturalised.

Following the leaf signs will bring visitors to the Vinery, once the site of a large greenhouse that has since collapsed. Excavation found that the very old vines were planted over a trench of sheep carcasses (a common practice in Victorian times!). Peaches grew against the tall walls next to the Vinery, which was also the site of the herb garden, and now contains many different herbs.

In the Gardener's Cottage, which was once the potting shed, is an oven formerly used for baking plant pots for the garden; next to the Cottage is the well still used for watering the garden.

In the centre of the garden is the Prospect; from here there are panoramic views over Port Isaac and Port Quin Bays. Four lighthouses are visible from here at night, Trevose to the south-west, Hartland to the north-east and two on Lundy Island out to sea to the left of Tintagel Head.

Location: Trelights, Port Isaac. north off B3314
Tel: (01208) 880 243
Facilities: Disabled Access, Lunches, afternoon teas, evening meals, freehouse tavern, Toilets, Dogs on leads, Plant Sales, Car & Coach Park.
N.B. Hotel on site.

Mary Newman's Cottage, Saltash

This tiny cottage is named after Sir Francis Drake's first wife who was purported to have lived here as a child.

The cottage was originally in a very dilapidated state but was restored by the Tamar Protection Society before being opened to the public in 1984.

The Victoria and Albert Museum has furnished the cottage with a collection of period furniture whilst to the rear of the house a typical cottage garden has been created with herbs, annuals and herbaceous plants. A collection of Armada roses has recently been planted to commemorate the 400th anniversary of the death of Sir Francis Drake. From the garden there are views of the River Tamar and Brunel's railway bridge.

Location: 48 Culver Road, Saltash, off Fore Street and Waterside
Tel: Tamar Protection Society (01752) 843 796
Facilities: Toilet, Dogs on leads,
Car & Coach park nearby.
Not suitable for disabled visitors.

Menacuddle Well

Menacuddle Well, St Austell

Mysterious Menacuddle lies hidden in a small wooded valley just to the north of St Austell. Access is via a small lane, easily missed, that plunges down from the main road into the valley.

Large beech trees tower overhead, giving dappled shade and lending a serene atmosphere to the tiny 15th century well tucked under an overhang of rock next to the fast flowing stream.

The well itself, a granite structure with gothic doorways, contains a spring the water of which formerly had a considerable reputation for healing "weakly children". It was also famous for divination or foretelling the future and for ensuing good fortune by throwing bent pins into the water.

Originally belonging to the priory of Tywardreath, the land eventually passed to the Rashleigh family who, according to Gilbert in 1820, carried out considerable planting interspersed with walks, rustic seats and ponds stocked with goldfish. At this period a rustic building was also to be found, all contributing to the "picturesque" effect.

By the 20th century the well had become extremely dilapidated but was restored by Sir Charles Sawle and both it and the land were given to the town in memory of his son killed during the First World War. It is now a public open space maintained by the Town Council.

Location: left off B3274 – just beyond viaduct

Mount Edgcumbe House & Park, Torpoint

The landscape at Mount Edgcumbe is the result of the inspiration of the Edgcumbe family over the last five hundred years.

The Deer Park was the first feature to be constructed – in 1529, when Piers Edgcumbe was granted a royal licence to empark part of the Rame peninsula. The family still lived at their old house at Cotehele, but were soon to move in 1553 to a newly built and much grander house that was to be known as Mount Edgcumbe. The avenue stretching nearly down to the ferry, and the area of garden round the house, were the earliest garden elements to be introduced.

By 1729, when the first map showing the grounds was made, the garden had developed into a complicated lay-out consisting of interconnecting serpentine walks and allées lined with clipped hedges.

However it was at this time that new ideas about gardening began to take hold and many estates were radically remodelled in the new style to imitate the classical landscapes seen on the Grand

The French Garden at Mount Edgcumbe

Tour, and those depicted on canvas by great artists of the day such as Claude Lorraine and Salvator Rosa.

Sir Richard, the 1st Baron, initiated many changes, including the building of the Folly and the Zig Zags, which were to become the most fashionable place to visit in the 18th century.

The next major changes to the garden were in 1779 when, due to the threat of invasion, hundreds of mature trees were felled to clear the view of advancing invaders. In view of this sacrifice, Sir George was elevated to become Viscount Mount Edgcumbe.

Undeterred by this felling, Sir George took advantage of the situation using the spaces to create the English Garden and place temples and classical urns throughout the garden. Often decorated with inspirational verse, these garden elements were meant to instil different moods ranging from sombre and dark to exuberant and inspired.

Richard, the second Earl, and his wife Sophia continued to expand the formal gardens with the construction of the Italian and French gardens, through to 1839. They also extended the Earl's Drive to take in the extensive prospect over the sea.

By the end of the 19th century the garden had become one of the finest landscaped gardens in England and, most unusually, due to the philanthropic nature of the 4th Earl, were open to the general public on Mondays.

This history of public access has continued and today the house and garden are owned jointly by Cornwall County Council and Plymouth City Council. Extensive work has had to be carried out on both house and garden (the house suffered a direct hit in the Second World War) and many of the built features and planting were in need of restoration.

The majority of the garden buildings, including the elegant Orangery, the Shell Grotto and temples have been restored and extensive work has been carried out to recreate the beautiful gardens.

The gardens now not only exhibit their former glory but continual development has taken place with new schemes such as the New Zealand garden (complete with geyser!) and an American garden with Carolina wild flowers and a pretty pergola.

Location: Cremyll, Torpoint
Tel: (01752) 822 236
Facilities: House Tea Room & Orangery Restaurant. Disabled Access, Dogs on leads, Toilets, Plant Sales, Car & Coach Park.

The Old Mill Herbary, Bodmin

The garden consists of approximately five acres of semi-wild terraced gardens on a steep south facing bank, and natural woodland walks interspersed with several islands and bridges alongside the unspoilt River Camel. The garden adjoins Helland Bridge which is listed in "The Patent Rolls" of 1381. Finished circa 1415, Helland is one of the best 15th century medieval bridges in Cornwall, notable for its four pointed arches

The medieval bridge at Helland, adjacent to the Old Mill Herbary

springing from water level and one rounded arch for the leat. In the Great Flood of 16th July 1847, caused by a waterspout on Davidstow Moor, the ensuing flood water sped down the Camel valley some 12 to 18 feet high and all the bridges with the exception of Helland Bridge and Wadebridge were swept away.

Research has established that Helland Bridge with its adjacent water mills were part of the Colquite Estate and are mentioned as early as June 1586, when the rent was 2/- per annum. There was a hop yard of one acre here in September 1653 and an orchard and herb garden in August 1775. The mill was fed by the leat and an undershot wheel was used for grinding corn and sawing wood. This was in use till around 1934, being demolished in 1939, but various relics and several large granite stones, troughs and mushrooms have been found and may be seen together with the large granite cider press (now a fountain).

In addition to the wide range of natural flora to be found throughout the garden, there are named displays of culinary, medicinal and aromatic herbs, shrubs, climbing and herbaceous plants. A recent addition is a small arboretum of approximately one and three-quarter acres in a level meadow alongside the river and bridge. The leat leads to a Bog Garden where there are fountains and a raised patio pond with aquatics, Koi and other fish. There are also two small raised alpine gardens and a camomile lawn around a Greek fertility theme.

The garden was started from the wild in 1984, being entirely created by the present owners themselves.

Location: Helland Bridge, Bodmin – off B3206
Tel: (01208) 841 206
Facilities: Toilet, Plant Sales, No Dogs, Car Park.

Penberth, St Buryan

Penberth lies 8 miles south-west of Penzance in a small valley leading to the picturesque Penberth Cove. The house and garden are approached through the stone arch of the gatehouse on the left.

The privately owned five-acre garden may be described as a path to the sea set in a rocky valley leading to the sea. From the terrace by the house is a magnificent view overlooking the garden with the sea in the background beyond the cove. Started in 1922 by Dr Vernon Favell, grandfather of the present owner, planting has been established amongst the massive natural boulders of this unusual and spectacular site. The cascading stream and swirling mill leat add a dimension of sound to the garden as well as supplying a setting for a collection of bog plants. The mild climate enjoyed by the garden enables tender plants to be grown, some of which were recommended by W. Arnold-Forster (author of "Trees and Shrubs for the Milder Counties") during the early days of the garden. Shelter from the salt-laden winds which sweep the valley is provided by a number of established trees, carefully sited so as not to obstruct the view to the sea beyond.

Following Dr Favell's death in 1936 the garden was maintained by Mrs Favell with the help of the late John Henry Chapple who left school at the age of 14 in 1923 to join the garden staff for all his working life. He became Head Gardener until his retirement in 1974. Mrs Favell's eldest son, the late Commander Richard Favell DSC RN, came to live at Penberth in 1955 and, over the next forty years, he developed and extended the garden down the valley towards the sea.

Daffodils, which were bred at this garden by Dr Vernon Favell and are still available include 'Logan Rock', 'Sweetness', 'Porth Chapel', 'Victorious' and 'Penberth'. Also growing in the garden are watsonias imported many years ago from South Africa, the orange coloured type flowering from October until January. Others with pink to cream shades flower at the more conventional time in summer to extend the display in this garden. Growing in what was the old orchard in 1922 is a collection of azaleas, magnolias and camellias including fine mature specimens of *Camellia japonica* 'Althaeiflora', planted in 1916, *C.j.* 'Mathotiana alba', *C.j.* 'Peach Blossom', *Camellia x williamsii* 'St. Ewe', *Azalea* 'Hino-mayo', *Azalea* 'Hinode-giri' and *Magnolia hypoleuca*.

The water garden is the oldest part of Penberth with two large tree ferns (*Dicksonia antarctica*) from which three sections each 2ft tall have been successfully removed and transplanted. A fine specimen of *Magnolia x soulangeana* 'Alba' and a *Rhododendron diaprepes* are features of this area. Growing in the mill stream is skunk cabbage (*Lysichiton americanus*) and nearby is a fine specimen of the low spreading azalea 'Gumpo Pink' which John Henry Chapple described as "cuddling the rocks". A carpet of *Vinca minor* makes good effective ground cover here.

The Rock Garden of massive boulders contains a collection of shrubs including many species of rhododendron and elaeagnus. A magnificent feature of this area is the *Puya berteroniana*, spectacularly producing steel blue flowers on a 6ft spike. This rare plant came originally from the Rectory garden of the late Canon Boscawen at Ludgvan. Commander Favell's eldest daughter came to live at Penberth in 1987 and is extending the garden still further up the valley.

Wild garlic at Pencarrow

Also in the garden is the Old Mill which is over a thousand years old. The land on which it stands is recorded as having been given to the monks of St Buryan in 943 by King Athelstone. Another historic feature is the "Queen's Road", named after Queen Elizabeth I who was reputed to have walked through the garden to the sea whilst staying at a neighbouring farm at the top of the hill. Penberth boasts its own Cornish Cross amongst the many interesting features in this fascinating garden.

Location: Penberth, St Buryan, Penzance – south of B3315
Facilities: Part Disabled Access, Cream Teas, Toilets, Occasional Plant Sales, No Dogs, Car Park near.

Pencarrow, Bodmin

Pencarrow lies at the foot of a valley near the little village of Washaway and is approached by a mile-long drive passing through an extensive plantation woodland and an ancient British encampment.

Although the estate has been owned by the Molesworth family and their descendants, the Molesworth St Aubyns since Elizabethan times, the present house dates from the mid 18th century.

The majority of the Grade II historic garden was designed and laid out between 1831 and 1855 by the notable statesman Sir William Molesworth. His first task was the construction of an Italian style garden in front of the house, complete with a central fountain, surrounded by elaborate parterres. (Interestingly, the latter, in spite of being grassed over, can still be picked out on aerial photographs.)

The enormous rockery was his next project, said to have been constructed with the assistance of his tenants, who were so annoyed that he had not been re-elected to parliament due to his radicalism that they proceeded to show their solidarity by carting large blocks of granite from Bodmin Moor.

A keen plantsman, he was the recipient of many of Veitch's plants, grown from seed brought back by the mid 19th-century plant hunters such as Douglas, Hooker and William Lobb (who was born on the Pencarrow estate, his father being an estate carpenter). Sir William planted the recently introduced conifers alongside the Long Drive and in the amenity woodlands that he was developing in the adjoining valley. A lake was constructed here and beyond it a fashionable "American" garden, originally containing only plants and trees emanating from the American continent.

It was at Pencarrow that the name Monkey Puzzle originated – a guest describing one of his new conifers (*Araucaria araucana*) said that the tree would puzzle a monkey!

Although many of his trees have since died of old age, some do survive, notably the very rare *Taxodium distichum* var. 'nutans', now the oldest known swamp cypress in Britain.

After Sir William's death, further planting was carried out by his widow and sister. Many of the fine trees of the present time were planted after the First World War by Sir Hugh Molesworth St Aubyn. He was succeeded by his son, Sir John, who was responsible for the lovely rhododendrons, camellias and azaleas that fill the garden with colour in the Spring.

During the Second World War Pencarrow suffered badly from neglect, in common with many other estates. Following the war, clearance and replacement planting was carried out including many broad-leaved trees such as oaks and maple varieties which give brilliant autumn colour.

In addition to carrying on the family tradition of planting conifers, of which nearly two hundred species and varieties are now represented in the garden, the present incumbent, Sir Arscott, has introduced hundreds more different rhododendrons, azaleas and tender shrubs.

A further dimension of the beauties of Pencarrow are the wild bluebells and garlic which carpet the woodlands in the spring.

Location: Washaway, Bodmin
Tel: (01208) 841 369
Facilities: Disabled Access, Teas, Toilets, Plant Sales, Dogs on leads, Car & Coach Park.
N.B. Garden maps available.

Penheale Barton, Launceston

Penheale Barton, in contrast to Penheale Manor's ancient roots (see below), has been developed since 1989. It is a small rectangular walled garden, not only with a wide variety of interesting herbaceous plants but also a section devoted to rhododendrons, camellias and magnolias.

A central island bed surrounded by lawns contains an extensive selection of flowering shrubs and heathers.

At the front of the house the terrace contains 'Ballerina' apple trees in pots, and the walls are clothed with roses, clematis and other climbing shrubs.

The owner has a particular fondness for salvias, of which there is a wide range of different varieties.

Location: Egloskerry, Launceston
Tel: (01566) 785 241
Facilities: Disabled Access, Teas, Toilets, Dogs on leads, Car & Coach Park nearby.

Penheale Manor Gardens, Launceston

In the 1920s Penheale was described by the scholar Ralph Edwards as follows:

"From this bleak upland a windy drive descends towards the house, which lies within walled gardens, screened by ancient trees, knarled, distorted, twisted into strange shapes and thickly covered with lichen borne on the salt-laden winds."

This feeling of age still persists and Penheale is indeed ancient, having first been described in the Domesday Survey. From this period until the reign of Henry VI the manor was owned by the Botterells, a war-like crew, given to wandering the country from one war to another with little interest in their base. After passing to the Hungerford family, the manor was eventually bought by the Grenvilles during the

The pool at Penheale Garden

reign of Elizabeth I. The first George Grenville rebuilt the medieval house but it was probably left to the subsequent Specott family to initiate work on the garden. The first known depiction of the garden is that in the romantically named Black Book of Spoure (dated from 1694) which shows a simple lay-out with steps (still existing) leading from the terrace.

The 18th and 19th centuries saw a series of owners and little garden activity until the house was bought by Norman Colville in 1920. He was deter-mined to rescue the house from its ruinous state and restore it to its former glory. The architect Sir Edwin Lutyens was employed to undertake the formidable task which included building a new wing.

At this time the formal garden was much smaller than it is now, consisting of an upper walled garden and a grassed courtyard with terraces dating from Elizabethan times still existed.

The Colvilles asked Lutyens to approach Gertrude Jekyll to design a formal garden to the west, in the area where a dilapidated building had been removed alongside the Lutyens wing. A design for a sunken rose garden was drawn out with box enclosing each bed and a border against the wall. Much of the planting in this area was carried out as planned with the broad herbaceous borders giving year long colour and interest. The eastern borders and enclosing yew hedges were Norman Colville's creation. The yews create a series of garden rooms, one of which incorporates a Greek style swimming pool. Herbaceous borders were also laid out along the terraces with a vista cut through the trees to obtain a view of Dartmoor. Lovely semi-circular granite steps lead down to a delightful pond over which there is a stunning view of the rhododendrons in the spring.

This delightful formal garden with its sense of containment and visual surprise is unique in Cornwall and forms a dramatic contrast with the valley gardens and parklands which exist elsewhere.

Location: Egloskerry, Launceston – east of A395
Tel: (01566) 785 486 and 693
Facilities: Disabled Access, Teas, Toilets, Plant Sales, Dogs on leads, Car & Coach Park.

Penjerrick, Falmouth

Situated one mile south of Budock Water, near Falmouth, Penjerrick House stands at the head of a sheltered valley, with south-easterly views between some magnificent trees and over the shrub-bordered lawn down the valley to the sea at Maenporth.

The property was bought by the Fox family in the early 19th century and was to be the summer home of this Quaker family. Robert Were Fox,

A glimpse of the sea at Penjerrick

Delphiniums in the walled garden at Penpol

born 1789, was the scientific representative of his generation. A mining expert, he wrote many scientific papers, invented navigational equipment, including the dipping needle compass, and carried out scientific experiments on the acclimatization of plants. He is credited with naturalizing over 300 species, many of which were brought to him by clients of the family shipping agency. Robert Were Fox married Maria Barclay and had three children, Anna Maria, Barclay and Caroline. Anna Maria at the age of 17 founded the Royal Cornwall Polytechnic Society in 1833. A keen writer, she kept a journal and although the greater part of it was destroyed after her death, a single volume survived, was published and proclaimed a great literary work. Barclay wrote a journal also which makes interesting reading about the life and times of this family. It was Robert Barclay Fox who was responsible for enlarging the existing cottages to make a house and, in the 1840s, for developing the gardens around it. He also laid out the entrance drive leading from the Lodge across the park to the north side of the house.

The present slate-hung house dates from 1935 after the earlier house became so dilapidated it had to be pulled down. A terrace walk across the front leads past the remains of what was a covered fernery and along the top of the garden. Winding paths lead off it through the plant collection which is laid out informally in the grass. The extensive collection of sub-tropical trees and shrubs includes original plants of early hybrid rhododendrons, crossed by Barclay Fox and by Mr Smith, one of his head gardeners. 'Penjerrick Cream' is one of the beautiful rhododendrons hybridized in this garden. There are massive specimens of *Dicksonia antarctica* (tree ferns) some reaching up to 5 metres high and with a girth of nearly two metres. There are also great clumps of bamboos, many camellias, azaleas and towering trees. The planted area extends on the far side of the road which, being sunken, does not interfere with the views down the garden. The road is crossed by a wooden bridge to a wilder area with its series of ponds, streams and luxuriant, lush, almost jungle-like atmosphere. This area contains a circular route running down between the four ponds which are gradually being restored.

Although Penjerrick was left to the National Trust by Mrs Janet M K Fox along with a substantial endowment, the endowment was not considered adequate and so sadly this bequest was turned down. It is now hoped to find another solution to keep this beautiful garden intact, and open to the public for their enjoyment.

Location: Budock, Falmouth
Tel: (01872) 870 105
Facilities: Plant Sales (sometimes), Dogs on leads.
N.B. Car parking on verge only.

Penpol House, Hayle

Penpol is in the south-west of Cornwall and the 16th-century house is surrounded by a three and a half acre garden that has been described by one writer as "a remarkable hidden jewel in Hayle that is a fine example of subtle planning and imaginative use of space".

Situated 150 feet up on a slope overlooking the Hayle estuary, shelter from the prevailing south-west and north-west salt laden winds from the sea is essential. This was formerly provided by many fine elm trees, but following the advent of Dutch Elm disease, three hundred of these had to be felled, leaving the garden very exposed. However, yew and fuchsia hedges remained along with box edging to many beds, and the trees and shrubs planted to replace the elms have now become established. Hedges and old walls divide the garden into a number of "pocket" gardens. Imaginatively placed granite troughs, staddle stones, cider press wheels, stone pillars and seats contribute to the distinctive character of each and are a reminder of the days when Penpol had a home farm.

The soil is alkaline, consequently the range of plants and trees differs from other Cornish gardens. Penpol has a reputation for delphiniums, and the Delphinium Society have supplied seed allowing a wide selection of colours and types to be raised.

The main area for the delphiniums is in the old walled garden, where the longest wall, running the length of the garden, affords a good backdrop as well as providing shelter from the wind. Here, in a wide box edged border, there are delphiniums in white with vari-coloured "bee" centres, pink and lavender, as well as the traditional dark and light blues. On two other walls old pear and apple espaliers have been retained, the beds beneath being planted with Naked Ladies (*Amaryllis belladonna*). The central area has been altered to create a water garden and a small bog area surrounded by shrub and patio roses. At the top end of the pool is a large terracotta vase in a bed surrounded with paeonies and geraniums. An escallonia hedge makes an evergreen backcloth, while a small lawn beyond contains another bed of delphiniums.

In recent years the delphiniums grown have included the red flowered *D. cardinale* and the yellow raised from seed from the Society. Sown in February, the seedlings are planted out in early April. Both colour forms begin to flower in late July and continue into mid to late October. The Cardinales are a fascinating reminder of the wild delphiniums seen on the border of Uganda and Kenya.

Other interesting features at Penpol include the Grey Garden, planned years ago for quiet grey colours. Now, however, the planting has been enlivened by the bright colours of a varied selection of plants and shrubs, including Lemon Verbena (*Aloysia triphylla*), *Chaenomeles japonica* and white Crinum lilies to name just a few. There is also a small complex of greenhouses in which an 80-year-old geranium fills one side of a 10 foot wall. Beyond this the garden opens out to its fullest extent with lawns, terraces and densely packed herbaceous borders. In May there are long rows of flag iris in yellow, blue, white and brown. Other smaller beds of *Iris unguicularis*, Snakeshead iris (*Hermodactylus tuberosus*) and beardless irises provide colour earlier in the season.

At the top of the garden there are more delphiniums and beds of dahlias, terrace beds of dianthus, rock roses and lavender, and a pool with kingcups bordering a croquet lawn. A wild garden containing trees such as poplar, beech, chestnut, alder and laburnum is hidden behind a hedge of pittosporum and hebes.

Roses are well represented; both climbing and rambling roses clamber over trellises. There is a hidden garden of 19th-century roses reminiscent of Redouté paintings, and also a formal rose garden where the largest group of well known roses is bordered by tall fuchsia hedges.

Location: Penpol Avenue, Hayle
Tel: (01736) 753 146
Facilities: Disabled Access, Teas, Toilets, Plant Sales
Charity Days, No Dogs, Car & Coach Park nearby.

Penrose, Helston

A little known National Trust property lying at the head of the lovely Loe Pool, Penrose estate as seen today dates mainly from the 18th century. Woods were planted, views from the house landscaped to make the most of the water feature and, for a time, even deer were kept in part of the park facing the house to the north.

Penrose House itself (not open to the public), dating from the 17th century, is set on a slope overlooking the Pool. In 1847 a bridge was built, not only as a practical feature but also to form an aesthetic feature in the landscape. Also built at this time was the bath house which has recently been restored. From the early years of the 18th century onwards it became fashionable in polite society to take cold baths in specially built bath houses. Here, although the pool itself was unheated, an open grate was installed to provide warmth.

The estate is notable for its variety of tree species; mixed woodlands give way near the sea to

Loe pool from Penrose

Monterey cypress (*Cupressus macrocarpa*) and Monterey pine (*Pinus radiata*). As in many other estates, these salt tolerant species were planted to give shelter to the less resistant species. Tree ferns and a bamboo grove can also be found nearer to the house.

After walking through the plantation, one reaches Loe Bar – a massive shingle bank separating the Pool from the sea. In folklore, the Bar was formed by the giant Tregeagle dropping a sack of sand during his act of penance; more prosaically, it has been formed by a combination of onshore and longshore drift, with flint shingle derived from an offshore deposit.

The bar is home to some interesting plants, especially the garden escapes such as *Fascicularia pitcairniifolia*, a member of the pineapple family, and the fleshy leaved Hottentot fig (*Carpobrotus edulis*) with its jewel bright flowers and (in a good summer) edible fruit.

Location: Off B3304 near Helston
Tel: National Trust, Lanhydrock

Penwarne, Mawnan Smith

Penwarne, the principal house in the parish of Mawnan, was in ancient times a Manor and Barton occupied by the Penwarne family (Richard Penwarne was MP for Penryn in 1620). The original mansion, of which some carved jamb stones and other pieces of stone remain, stood where the stables and barton are now and seems to have been built in the early 14th century. There was also a free chapel, the ruins of which were extant in 1690; the stone from the chapel was said to have been used to form the walls of the Chapel Garden and the tower by the pond was built from the stone to make a "cold room". The present Penwarne house was built in 1760 and the garden was laid out by the Reverend M M Peters in about 1850.

The gardens lie to the south and west of the house and provide a completely secluded setting for many magnificent mature specimen trees, rhododendrons, camellias, magnolias and other rare and tender shrubs. Snowdrops, daffodils and bluebells carpet the ground in the spring underneath the larger shrubs and trees.

There are two ponds fed by springs and various streams running down the garden. There are ornamental ducks on the top pond and both ponds are surrounded by tree ferns and water-loving plants.

Apart from the war years – when the garden, except for the kitchen garden, was largely neglected, the main lawn being used for grazing in 1945 – each successive owner of Penwarne has been a keen gardener and has enhanced and introduced many exotic plants from all over the world. The present owners have cleared large areas of laurel and *Rhododendron ponticum* and replanted with a vast selection of interesting and unusual shrubs.

Although the paths are quite narrow and steep, which makes the shrub areas unsuitable for wheelchairs, disabled visitors may enjoy the spectacular view from the classical Georgian house towards the sea; the walled garden is also accessible.

Location: Mawnan Smith, Falmouth
Tel: (01326) 250 325
Facilities: Limited access for Disabled, Toilets, No Dogs, Car Park.

Penzance, Bolitho Gardens

These gardens, presented by Thomas Bolitho, were opened in 1916 for the benefit of those returning from the Great War and contained a granite colonnade above walled and terraced planting beds. Known locally as the Italian Gardens, they also contained mementoes of the wars including weapons from the Crimean and Boer wars. From the gardens there are beautiful views of St Michael's Mount and the bay.

The gardens were completely destroyed by the sea during a great storm on the 8th March 1962; the site now contains a children's play area and flower beds.

Location: Town centre, Penzance
Tel: Penwith District Council (01736) 62341

An early 20th century post card of Morrab Gardens

Penzance, Morrab Gardens

Morrab, from the Cornish for "sea-shore", was purchased by Penzance Corporation in 1888, specifically for use as a public park. The development of Penzance as a holiday resort was proceeding apace and the Council, as many others at that time, was keen to be seen to provide amenities for the public (referred to by Trevelyan as "municipal socialism").

Tenders for the garden design were advertised nationally and a £21 prize was offered to the successful designer. The winner was Reginald Upcher, a landscape gardener from London. His design, based on a series of winding paths interspersed with irregularly shaped beds, was faithfully carried out, as can be seen from the original plan still surviving in the County Record Office. A garden for the blind, a revolutionary concept at that time, was also suggested by the architect.

The entrance path was flanked by an avenue of cordylines, depicted on many early postcard views and which are now large and ancient.

Today, Morrab is a treasure house of tender and rare plants, some of enormous size, including a cordyline over 2 feet in diameter. Many New Zealand plants are present – sophoras with their bright yellow flowers, together with *Cassinia fulvida* and a border of libertias.

Interesting fruit can also be seen, such as those of *Myrtus ugni* and, in favourable years, the bananas (*Ensete ventricosum*). Another curious fruit is the

Japanese Bitter Orange (*Poncirus trifoliata*), the stems of which are covered with rather ferocious spines.

These exotic gardens have most successfully realized the hopes of one writer in 1889 – "When the sea is lashing over the celebrated promenade, these sheltered gardens will form a pleasant retreat".

Location: Penzance, near to town centre.

Penzance, Penlee Memorial Park

Unlike Morrab Garden, which was intended from its inception in the late 19th century to be a public park, Penlee Memorial Park started life as a private garden surrounding a substantial house. Bought by the Council in 1945 as a memorial to the fallen in World War II, the original intention for the walled memorial garden was to include plants grown only

Autumn colour at Pine Lodge

in the British Empire which were to be of "no cost to the Borough Council"! The rest of Penlee was, however, already well furnished with mature trees and shrubs planted by its previous owner Alfred Branwell.

The walled garden is laid out as a series of small lawns surrounded by dwarf box. These act as a foil to the exuberant growth covering the tiny chapel. Many beautiful and interesting tender shrubs and climbers clothe the walls including unusual fuchsias, bomarea and *Asarina erubescens*. At the entrance to the garden the rare *Vallea stipularis* is covered with pretty pink flowers during the Spring.

The rest of the garden is also full of beautiful, rare and fascinating plants, every one an exclamation mark!

Location: Penzance, off Morrab Road

Pine Lodge Gardens, St Austell

Pine Lodge Gardens are located on part of the Cuddra Estate just to the east of St. Austell, the land being associated with the Rashleigh family

during the 19th century. Several noteworthy trees survive in the woodlands and parkland; an 8-metre *Arbutus unedo*, *Pinus montezuma* and *P. patula*, a beautiful *Cedrus libani* and many different Quercus. The garden now covers over 30 acres, with woodlands providing cover for early snowdrops, drifts of bluebells, aconites and anemones. Alpine plants include the lovely celmisias from New Zealand and miniature iris and cyclamen from Crete. Herbaceous borders show the famous blue meconopsis and other varieties in red, white and yellow. Other herbaceous plants include the rare *Myosotidium hortensia* with its blue flowers from the Chatham Islands, over 60 varieties of hardy geraniums and large groups of hardy orchids. Shrubberies feature not only rhododendrons, camellias, magnolias, pieris and azaleas, but sycopsis, daphnes, telopea, cestrum, myoporum and many others. A part of the arboretum provides a splendid show of the bark of *Betula jacquemontii* and *Prunus serrula* against the blue *Cedrus atlantica* 'Glauca'.

In 1993 a 4-acre pinetum was planted with over 80 varieties of firs ranging from the ground hugging *Microbiota decussata* to the ultimately 200 feet high giant *Sequoiadendron giganteum*. Water features in the garden include ponds with Koi carp and marsh gardens with the giant *Gunnera manicata*, candelabra primulas and many waterside iris. A wildlife pond sustains a wonderful range of dragonflies and other aquatic life. During 1994 a larger lake was added to the garden and an old 8-acre conifer plantation has been replaced by new plantings of a collection of native trees for future generations to enjoy.

Many rare and tender plants are held in the garden, including the National Collection of Grevilleas from Australia. In all over 5,500 plants are in the garden, all clearly labelled.

The most recent addition is a formal garden planted in a circle combining all the colours of the spectrum. The emphasis when planning the garden has been very much towards colour combinations and co-ordination. The autumn colour is spectacular – a small grove of acers, cercis, parrotia, sorbus and stewartia can then be seen in all their brilliance. The plants are labelled so take pen and paper when you visit to note down your favourites in this superb "all-year-round garden".

Location: Off the A390 between Holmbush and Tregrehan, St Austell
Tel: (01726) 73500
Facilities: Disabled Access, Toilets, Plant Sales, No Dogs, Car & Coach Park.
N.B. Teas on charity days only.

Pinetum, Calstock

Pinetum is a two-acre private garden overlooking the River Tamar on the border between Cornwall and Devon. The house faces due north with spectacular views over the Tamar valley to nearby Gunnislake. The garden is south-facing, and is therefore able to support many tender plants.

Pinetum was established approximately twenty-five years ago from what had been a small market garden. The plot was extensively planted with many unusual pines, conifers, acers, abies, eucalypts, birches, prunus, cornus and also many species and hybrid rhododendrons, camellias and azaleas. More recently a large number of the trees and shrubs have been under-planted with herbaceous plants, ferns and shade-loving plants.

Meandering through the trees are "natural" pathways creating enjoyable and secretive walks with many interesting features appearing in their own compartments. During the last three years the garden pond has been developed to such an extent that it now supports many forms of wildlife including newts and frogs. Marsh marigold (*Caltha*) and various rushes have been added for the benefit of emerging damsel and dragon flies, and different types of water lily grow in the pool, which is flanked by attractive flower beds.

At various points the pathways lead through arches entwined with clematis, roses and honey-suckles. A large raised bed has been formed containing a selection of heather, dwarf conifers and various grasses under-planted with many miniature bulbs for spring colour. Other recent additions have been a rockery and a gazebo (made from hand-spun fibreglass) with adjacent flower beds supporting various climbers. Next to the conservatory at the rear of the house is a large patio area with colourful tubs, hanging baskets and a water feature, and bordered by patio roses and troughs planted with alpines.

Because of the unusual range of both evergreen and deciduous trees the garden has become the natural home to many birds. A collection of 20 bird nest boxes has been built up and virtually all of these have been occupied this year. During the nesting season the adult and young birds deal with the not-so-welcome aphids, slugs and snails. The garden is run organically and nearly all garden debris (branches, leaves, grass, weeds, etc.) is shredded, composted and consequently re-cycled.

Pinetum is different from many local gardens which tend to look at their best only in spring. This is mainly due to the mixed planting of deciduous and evergreen trees which give dramatic seasonal changes of colour and texture in their new growth, bark, flowers and cones, particularly in autumn.

As with all gardens there are many new ideas in the pipeline to improve and create more compartments and to make the garden more enchanting.

Location: Harewood, Calstock – through Albaston past Calstock Parish Church
Tel: (01822) 832 379
Facilities: Disabled Access, Teas, Plant Sales, Toilets, No Dogs, Parking in lane.

Poldowrian, Helston

Valerie and Peter Hadley came to Poldowrian in 1965, but it was not until 1970, when they had sold their dairy herd, that they started to make their garden.

Between the house and the cliff was a field, bounded on the west by a stream with willows and thorns, and, beyond, a thick jungle of gorse and bramble. The first stage was to hack a path to the cliff, clearing some of the gorse, but leaving much of it among the colourful heather banks. In the clearings of the little wood many camellias, rhododendrons and other shrubs were planted wherever the spade did not encounter rock or blue clay. Trees were then inter-planted amongst the wood, including beech, hoheria, amelanchier and liquidambar.

Several yards of the field were fenced off, and here were planted golden macrocarpa, chamaecyparis, rowan, larch, whitebeam, ash and hollies.

As the upper part of this small valley was boggy, a pond with an island was dug out, and over the years many more plants have been added on each bank. At the bottom, where the garden reaches the Cornwall coastal footpath, clematis has been trained over large rock faces and up various trees. More rhododendrons, camellias, cistus and ceanothus meet the astonished eyes of cliff walkers as they come down to cross the little stream.

To the west of the stream, at the bottom, a small pinery was planted to provide shelter from the gales – these include *Pinus radiata*, *P. muricata*, *P. contorta* and *P. maritima*, and on the east side two Japanese umbrella pines (*Sciadopitys verticillata*), a Norway maple and various shrubs including *Viburnum carlesii*, *Azalea* 'Addy Wery', *Camellia* 'Adolphe Audusson' and *Rhododendron macabeanum*.

Many years later, the west-facing slope of the lower valley was cleared of scrub and planted with low shrubs. From the seat at the top one looks down over this "horseshoe garden" (so called from the shape of its surrounding path) and away south across the bay to the Lizard.

In 1994 a small ornamental pond and a rocky bog garden were added near the house – a pleasant place to sit and watch the fish as the water gushes down. Trees are still being added where possible, taking care to leave the garden as a blend of the wild and the cultivated. Although only 25 years old, it has already matured enough to give pleasure to its creators and their many visitors. "Magical" is the word most often used to describe it, and there is indeed something magical about Poldowrian, where time itself seems to stand still. Perhaps archaeology has something to do with it, for here much evidence of prehistoric habitation has been found. Relics of these prehistoric inhabitants are on display in the Poldowrian Museum of Prehistory, which attracts many interested visitors.

Location: Coverack, Helston – off Lizard Road B3293
Tel: (01326) 280 460
Facilities: Part Disabled Access, Plant Sales, No Dogs.

Polgwynne, Feock

The house and garden at Polgwynne, Feock, lie within what was originally the walled productive gardens of the adjacent Porthgwidden.

Beautifully situated overlooking the Fal estuary,

Polgwynne garden

Porthgwidden was the home in the 19th century of Canon Philpotts. His passion was for his greenhouses, built in 1850, which still exist in good condition. Growing not only vines, melons and cucumbers, he also indulged himself in his precious orchids. He invented a method of heating the greenhouses which involved building an air chamber between the two houses with a complex series of drains to eliminate draughts and warm the air.

Equally passionate philosophically, he advocated gardening for the common man to balance the materialistic attitudes of the Industrial Revolution. As a result of this, he organised the first ever exhibition of the Royal Horticultural Society outside London in 1859 – its aim to show the cottager how he could improve his condition and bring comfort to his family.

When Philpotts retired in 1874 he converted a large part of the grounds into the present walled garden.

Originally a fine garden, by the 1960s it had deteriorated and the owners put it down to grass. In 1966 Mr and Mrs Davey purchased the property and thereafter took great pleasure in redesigning and laying out a new garden. Some original plantings survive including an enormous female *Gingko biloba*, reputed to be the oldest in Britain.

The garden is laid out as a series of interconnecting spaces each with a special feature. A small formal pool lies tucked away under a steep bank, whilst an old well feeds a rill which winds its way through the lower garden. The fine potting sheds at the back of the range of greenhouses provide further visual interest, and changes of level contribute to the feeling of variety.

Many rare and beautiful plants are to be found in the main garden. In contrast a quiet path winds its way through woodland to the peaceful water's edge of the Fal estuary.

Location: Feock, Truro – take Feock road off A39
Tel: (01872) 862 612
Facilities: Part Disabled Access, Toilets, No Dogs.
N.B. Teas & Plant Sales on charity days only.

Porthpean, St Austell

The house, at one time the Dolphin Inn, was built towards the end of the 18th century. Additions were made in the latter part of the 19th century when the core of the garden was also laid out.

The stunning position of the house, one of the few gardens in Cornwall at the very edge of the sea, means that the garden is very exposed, but nevertheless it does not seem to suffer unduly. The three acres contain a variety of planting including a magnificent collection of over 250 varieties of

Porthpean

camellia started by Maurice Petherick after the Second World War. The best camellias are to be found in the more sheltered areas underneath mature trees. Summer colour is given by roses and a wide variety of shrubs and herbaceous plants. One gable end is entirely covered by the "Wedding Day" rose which flowers happily in the teeth of the gales.

A particularly charming feature is the thatched summerhouse garlanded with a *Clematis montana*. The summerhouse provides a wonderful view of the sea towards Black Head.

Of particular interest are two miniature camellias developed in America and also a semi-double deep pink cultivar found as a chance seedling at Porthpean which has been named after the garden.

A very large free-standing *Magnolia grandiflora* and a huge *Dicksonia antarctica* are also to be found here, the latter reputed to be the furthest east in the county.

The garden is remarkable for its breathtaking carpet of primroses in the spring and a very impressive *Acacia pravissima* which has raced away and has reached 25 feet in only six years.

Location: Lower Porthpean, St Austell – off B3273
Tel: (01726) 72888
Facilities: Part Disabled Access, Toilets, Dogs on leads, Car & Coach Park.

The newly restored garden at Prideaux Place

Prideaux Place, Padstow

Prideaux, a house of rather surprising castellated frontage and mock fortifications, overlooks the lovely Camel Estuary just to the west of Padstow.

Earliest depictions of the house and garden are by Edmund Prideaux at the end of the 17th century. A keen artist, he not only produced many drawings of his own property, but also travelled round Cornwall, Devon and Norfolk sketching many great houses of the period. (This invaluable record still exists, copies of which are in the County Record Office.)

In 1720 Prideaux laid out very formal gardens with an obelisk, a maze-like wilderness and a temple; of these only the temple now remains. He and his son also constructed the crenellated entrance gates and saluting platform which overlooks the deer park. The classical antiquities to be found on the terrace were brought back by Edmund from his Grand Tour to Rome; he was also responsible for the construction of the grotto niche surrounded by large boulders.

The 19th century saw great changes to the garden and many of the early works were swept aside to make way for ambitious projects. Crenellated footbridges leading to the raised walk were introduced and a small sunken garden and shell house were built by the Reverend Charles

Glyn Prideaux-Brune, whose watercolour design for the sunken garden dated 1878 is in the house.

More recently, due to much of the garden having fallen into disrepair, extensive restoration has been undertaken. Some parts were impenetrable, in other areas treasures such as the shell house and temple could barely be discerned amongst the undergrowth.

The Victorian sunken garden, designed by Charles Glyn Prideaux-Brune and depicted on a water-colour of 1878, has been restored with the help of Cornwall Gardens Trust. Careful study of old photographs and a site survey has enabled restoration to proceed. In the area of the sunken pool, lawns were re-laid and flowerbeds and ornamental pots replaced. The particularly charming Grade II gothic dairy and the rustic wall on the Green Walk also date from this period.

Location: Padstow — above the town
Tel: (01841) 532 411
Facilities: Part Disabled Access, Teas, Toilets, Dogs on leads, Car Park.
N.B. Limited parking usually available in grounds.
Optional tours of house extra.

Probus Gardens, Truro

Probus Gardens represent a unique opportunity for the public to view a wide variety of plants in different settings, and to examine the results of a host of gardening techniques.

An amusing sculpture at Probus

Established in 1969 by Cornwall County Council and opened in 1972 as the County Demonstration Garden, the seven and a half acre site shows what can best be grown under typical Cornish conditions and demonstrates new ways to approach gardening.

Mesembryanthemums at Probus

In spite of its location on an exposed ridge, the imaginative use of attractive hedges and ingenious planting schemes ensures a flourishing diversity of plants.

The site is undergoing constant refurbishment with major new exhibits such as a series of separate gardens based on exotic, hardy or wind resistant species.

Displays also show examples of gardening techniques – the effects of fertilizer, manures, mulching and pruning can all be examined in detail.

Plant surgeries and adult education courses are also available and exciting craft, art and gardening exhibitions are a regular feature.

Location: Probus near Truro – on south of A390
Tel: (01726) 882 597 Fax: (01726) 883 868
Facilities: Disabled Access, Cafe, Shop, Plant Centre, Toilets, No Dogs, Car & Coach Park.

Roseland House, Chacewater

The present garden of about one acre is situated in the old mining village of Chacewater. Roseland House itself dates from sometime in the 1700s and became a Mine Captain's house during the mining boom of the early 1800s, with most of the house's Victorian features being added around 1840. Both the house and garden had become neglected by the time the present owners arrived in 1983, and nothing remains of the Victorian gardens apart from an early monkey puzzle tree and a few specimens of yew which were originally planted as ornamental shrubs but have now become trees.

The history of mining in the area is extensive and goes back to the Bronze Age. This means that the soil, which is neutral to acid, is also high in arsenic, lead, copper and zinc, which causes problems with some plant types, notably rhododendrons.

The garden now is mainly mixed herbaceous and shrub planting. Climbers are of special interest; because of the relatively mild climate a large range of climbers can be found in the garden. Shrubs have been planted mainly to provide support for the 75 varieties of clematis. There is also a special emphasis on plants with scented flowers or foliage. Luckily, a Victorian conservatory (c. 1840) has survived which enables a wide range of plants to be grown. The scented leaf pelargoniums do well inside, as do several passion flowers and other tender climbers.

The top of the garden is still orchard and home to free-range hens. Some of the older trees are probably originals from the 1800s, with several unusual apple varieties still persisting. Under the trees there are many daffodils and around the edges several large rambling roses.

This is very much a family garden, where space for football and guinea pigs is as important as the plants, and ideas to save time find favour over more traditional gardening practices!

Location: take Chasewater road off A390 west of Truro
Facilities: Teas, Toilets, Plant Sales, Dogs on leads.
N.B. Car & Coach Park nearby.

St. Just-in-Roseland Church

During the 1920s H.V. Morton wrote of St. Just "I have blundered into a garden of Eden that cannot be described in pen or paint. There is a degree of beauty that flies so high that no net of words or no snare of colour can hope to capture it, and of this order is the beauty of St. Just-in-Roseland..."

This may seem high flown praise, but the beauty of the church in its creekside setting remains little changed over the passing years.

It may seem curious to include a churchyard in a book about gardens, but the churchyard, as well as having an intrinsic beauty in its setting and its historic church, also contains many exotic trees and shrubs brought back by John Garland Treseder in the last years of the 19th century.

The creekside with its sheltered and beneficial climate proved an ideal resting place for the plants and also for the nursery he subsequently developed. His work has been continued with later plantings of such species as fuchsia, griselinia, a rare pink form of the Chilean myrtle, camellia and arbutus amongst many others. The mature palms clustered around the ancient church are particularly arresting, and the gunnera "swamp" forms another unexpected feature. The ancient holy well of St Just, the water of which is still used for baptism, lies just outside the churchyard.

In 1984 further ground was planted up within the extension of the burial ground and a more recent development has been the Memorial Garden on the opposite side of the road.

Location: St. Just-in-Roseland – off A3078
Ref: In Search of England – H.V. Morton

St Michael's Mount, Marazion

The most famous of all attractions to visitors down the centuries, St Michael's Mount still tantalises the traveller with its romantic setting, rising out of the ever changing sea. Sometimes silhouetted

St Just-in-Roseland Church

The early walled garden at St Michael's Mount

blackly against the shining sands, at other times shrouded in mist or being battered by enormous waves, the Mount is always beautiful and has provided the inspiration for innumerable artists, including J M W Turner.

Most people probably have a preconceived image even before they arrive of what the Mount will be like. However, most are somewhat surprised to find that its apparent barrenness has been modified by substantial and diverse planting.

Until the end of the 19th century the rock was indeed devoid of much in the way of planting, although interestingly the Celtic for the Mount – Carrek Los y'n Cos – means "Hoary Rock in the Wood". (This is said to derive from the fact that Mount's Bay was originally wooded and has been inundated by the sea during the historical period.)

The earliest feature to survive is a small walled garden, perhaps an early herb garden to serve the monks, but more likely an 18th-century addition by the St. Aubyn family. Most of the planting structure seen today is the work of the first Lord St. Levan from 1887 onwards.

He also laid out shrubberies and planted many shelter trees. The delightful dairy, its design derived from one at Glastonbury Abbey, also dates from the late 19th century.

Today the scene is quite different – the eastern side of the Mount could be described as one vast

and precipitous rock garden! It is laden with plants growing out of every crack and crevice. One can only imagine the herculean labour involved in bringing soil from the mainland and hauling it up and down the precipice in order to create planting pockets for the rare and tender plants that flourish so astonishingly. Here one can see aloes, yuccas, succulents; the gardeners have to use mountaineering climbing harnesses in order to plant and tend all these amazing specimens.

Other delights to be seen are the drifts of bluebells and daffodils on the lower slopes during the spring, and in contrast in the autumn, fiery Red Hot Pokers (*Kniphofia rooperi*). More conventional rock garden shrubs such as heathers and junipers can also be seen in the mixed shrubbery.

Azaleas, rhododendrons and camellias can be found on the north slope leading down to the village and a small herb garden has been created near the village. The herb garden has been based on the concept of a medieval monastery garden, and exhibits plants with both ornamental and medicinal value.

Over the past twenty years the garden has developed astonishingly, especially in view of the dramatic climatic and physical conditions which represent a unique and challenging situation.

NB The gardens are open during the Garden Festival 1 April - 3 May every day and at weekends for charities, who charge an admission fee.

Location: Marazion, half mile walk across causeway, ferry boat when causeway closed.
Tide and ferry information (01736) 710 265
Tel: (01736) 710 507
Facilities: Unsuitable for Disabled, Plant Sales, No Dogs, Cafe and NT restaurant.

Springfield Farm Garden, Allet

Springfield Garden was started in 1980. It is planted purely for the owners' pleasure on retirement, and consists of two and a half acres of shrubs, herbaceous, bog and pond plants. There is a section of woodland containing magnolias, camellias and rhododendrons, under-planted with daffodils, erythroniums, ajuga and several more unusual plants. (Trilliums have been tried but unfortunately squirrels dig them up!) Just above the woodland section there is a natural pond containing principally water lilies and aponogeton. The pond is bordered by herbaceous plants and shrubs. The rest of the garden contains a mixture of trees and shrubs, several of them unusual.

The owner welcomes visitors to the garden, but please telephone first!

The pool at Springfield, Allet

Location: 3.5 miles from Truro on the Perranporth road B3284
Tel: (01872) 540 492
Facilities: Disabled Access, Teas, Toilets, Plant Sales (for charity), Dogs on leads, Car & Coach Park.

Tehidy, Camborne

Just a short distance from Camborne, Tehidy Country Park can be found nestled in a valley behind the wild and windswept cliffs of the north coast.

Once part of the vast estate of the Bassett tin mining family, remnants of its glorious past are still to be seen. Stockdale, in 1824, wrote:

"Tehiddy, when viewed from Carn Brea Hill, appears like a well cultivated garden in the midst of a sterile desert. Its spreading woods are beheld with additional delight from the contrasted scenery of the surrounding country, where the face of nature has been robbed of all ornament, and the earth scattered over its surface in the pursuit of ore."

The house and gardens were started in 1734 when Thomas Edwards of Greenwich was employed to design a new building to replace a smaller existing mansion. Consisting of a central

block with four detached pavilions, the house overlooked a lake that had been purposely made to enhance the prospect. Extensive tree planting was carried out, particularly to the north, in order to shelter the house from the sea winds. A parkland was laid out to the south of the house and cascades and temples were to be found amongst the woodlands.

The Bassett family lived in considerable style thanks to their mining interests, carrying out various changes to the house and gardens throughout the 18th and 19th centuries. By the outbreak of the First World War, a combination of reduced income and profligate expenditure combined with a reduction in manpower led, as in so many other cases, to the break-up of the estate.

The house was bought as a TB hospital but was almost immediately burnt to the ground, leaving it a mere shadow of its former glory. A replacement building of considerably less architectural merit was erected, and the gardens and estate gradually became overgrown during the ensuing years.

The grounds were purchased by the County Council in 1983 for use as a country park, following which there have been a number of exciting discoveries, such as the Rose Garden hidden under acres of undergrowth.

The 18th century cascade at Tehidy

The lovely cascade still survives and the woodlands provide a fine location for informal recreation. There are numerous events throughout the year, ranging from wildlife events to outdoor education and woodland trails for bikes, ponies, orienteering and pedestrians.

Location: Off A30 near Pool, Camborne
Tel: Cornwall County Council (01209) 714494

Trebah, Mawnan Smith

On the wooded northern slopes of the Helford River lies Trebah, one of the most beautiful properties in Cornwall. It is no pampered, pristine, prissy garden with rows of clipped hedges, close-mown striped lawns and daily raked paths. Here is a magnificent old, wild, enchanted Cornish dream world – the end product of 100 years of inspired and dedicated creation, followed by forty years of mellowing neglect and ten years of love and restoration.

Chusan palms at Trebah

"Like a corner of the Himalayas only better cared for", Trebah is the home of Major and Mrs. Anthony Hibbert. The family has given the estate to the Trebah Garden Trust, an independent charity, to ensure the garden will remain open for the enjoyment of the public for ever.

The 26-acre sub-tropical ravine garden falls 60 metres down to the private beach on the Helford River. A stream winding down through water gardens with waterfalls and Koi carp is flanked with carpets of arums and candelabra primula and there are two acres of blue and white hydrangeas. Hundred-year-old rhododendrons and magnolias overhang glades of giant gunnera and tree ferns. The side curtains of magnificent beeches and copper beeches climb the steep walls of the ravine, and the backdrop of the Helford River and the distant Bosahan hills form a theatrical set of extraordinary beauty.

There are mature plants and trees collected from all over the world by the Fox family of Falmouth, who were justly famous as garden designers and plant lovers of extraordinary genius. Massive plantings of rare bamboos and huge tree

The water gardens at Trebah

Tregrehan, St Austell

In spite of being only one mile from the sea, Tregrehan's location within the sides of a shallow valley provides good protection from the westerly gales.

Whilst under the ownership of the Edgcumbe family, the early gardens were developed around the house with a deer park to the south. The estate passed to the Caerlyon family in the 16th century, and from the early 19th century onwards William Carlyon began planting many of the new varieties of trees being brought into the country by explorers such as David Douglas and the Lobb brothers. Carlyon and his son Edward were particularly interested in conifers. These original plantings form one of Tregrehan's glories, having reached exceptional size, and now include many of the country's "champion" trees as noted by the late Alan Mitchell, the acclaimed dendrologist, in his extensive research throughout Britain on behalf of the Forestry Commission.

Edward Carlyon was at the forefront of fashion, not only building the magnificent range of greenhouses but also, in 1845, engaging W A Nesfield to set out a formal parterre to the front of the house. Although the parterre was dismantled in 1970, plans still survive and it can also be picked out on early aerial photographs.

The Carlyons continued to run the garden with extensive plantings up until World War II. The garden then became relatively neglected until the mid 1970s, when Miss Gillian Carlyon started clearing work. A talented propagator, inspired by the collection of old camellias, she undertook a programme of hybridization resulting in a wide variety of new and excellent cultivars. New cultivars from other sources were also brought in at this time, thus extending the collection. Amongst the large number of camellias bred at the garden are 'Tristrem Carlyon' with perfect pom-poms of rose madder, 'Nijinsky' a semi-double brilliant pink, and 'E T R Carlyon' a beautiful white double.

Within the garden are a number of interesting features – these include a yew walk and the lovely greenhouses (which have recently been extensively restored). Within the greenhouses can be seen a fine collection of tender 'Vireya' rhododendrons and various colour forms of the spectacular Chilean bellflower (*Lapageria rosea*).

In contrast to the exotics within the greenhouse is the valley floor where the largest and most remarkable conifers flourish.

The tallest tree in the garden is *Picea sitchensis* (150ft) whilst others worth noting are Japanese firs (*Abies firma*), podocarpus species and a number of

ferns from New Zealand, Australia and Tasmania place the visitor in the heart of a sub-tropical rain forest, while at the top of the garden is a Mediterranean setting with bananas, agapanthus, echiums, dasylirion, yuccas, aloes, agaves, mesembryanthemum, pelargoniums, beschorneria, puya and even an Australian "Black Boy" (*Xanthorrhoea preisii*).

While Trebah will always be a mecca for the plantsman, the policy of the Trust is to develop and maintain it first and foremost as a natural, wild, enchanted garden of timeless beauty.

At the same time, Trebah remains a garden where children are made to feel welcome. Tarzan's Camp provides a wonderful natural play area within the enfolding arms of a huge Western red cedar (*Thuja plicata*). The Paraglide is easily the most popular attraction for children, and is training whole battalions of the young to become parachutists! A series of trails, the Trebah Trail, the Time Trail and others, are available for all age groups.

Location: Mawnan Smith – follow the brown and white signs
Tel: (01326) 250 448
Facilities: Part Disabled Access, Shop, Plant Sales, Coffee Shop, Toilets, Dogs on leads, Car & Coach Park

The fountain in the walled garden at Tregrehan

extremely large pines and hemlocks. Growing epiphytically as they do in the wild are two self sown seedlings of Western hemlock *(Tsuga heterophylla)*, arising out of an old pine log.

Alan Mitchell has in the past described Tregrehan as a "Treasure house of outsize rarities"; it still continues to be so, and further exciting developments continue with the keen plant-hunting interest of the current custodian, Tom Hudson.

Location: St Blazey Gate off A390
Tel: (01726) 814 389
Facilities: Part Disabled Access, Teas, Toilets, Plant Sales, No Dogs.
Ample Car & Coach Park.

Tregullow, Redruth

The house and grounds at Tregullow lie adjacent to Scorrier House and are associated with the Williams family, well-known for their gardening passions for over a century.

With their linkages to other great 19th-century gardens of Cornwall – Caerhays and Burncoose – the Williamses of Tregullow were well placed not only to receive many interesting plants brought into the country by the plant hunters, but also to benefit from the hybridization developments taking place. Many of these plants still exist in the shrubberies underlying the informal woodlands surrounding the house, and are now being restored to their former glory after becoming overgrown.

Although the two large walled gardens are not used as such today, one may still discern interesting remnants of the old heating system adjacent to the extremely high walls of the smaller walled garden.

The ornamental woodlands gradually merge into more natural woodlands to the south and towards the valley where some fine clumps of mature conifers may be seen. Of particular interest in this area is Prince Albert's yew *(Saxegothaea conspicua)*, a rare species named in honour of Prince Albert, consort of Queen Victoria, after the province from which he came. Introduced by William Lobb in 1847, this tree is very likely from the original seed, William having worked at the neighbouring Scorrier before his travels and presumably keeping in touch with his former employers.

The house itself overlooks an open lawn at the bottom of which runs the disused Portreath tramway built in 1804 by the Williams family to take ore from their extensive mines at St Day, northwards to the sea at Portreath.

(Incidentally, the tramway systems of Cornwall have recently been renovated to provide walkways and visitors' information along their length and one of the coaches, specially designed for "the great and the good", can be seen at the Royal Cornwall Museum in Truro.)

Location: Off B3298 near Scorrier
Tel: (01209) 820 775
Facilities: Disabled Access, Teas, Plant Sales, Dogs on leads, Car Park.

Trehane, Probus

There are many houses called Trehane in Cornwall. The name is thought to date from the Bronze Age and to mean "The House of Han".

This particular site has a history dating back at least until the 13th century. The present mansion was started in 1700, using, unusually for Cornwall, bricks which are thought to have come from clay found at Trewithen.

The basic structure of the garden was in compartments formed by the impact of the great wall of the homestead on the bottom of the slopes.

By the middle of the 19th century the estate had passed to a Captain Pinwill, who was particularly interested in natural history and who became a great gardener, much influenced by his friendship with the Reverend Boscawen of Lamorran.

The tradition of spring gardens with trees and shrubs had not yet invaded Cornwall but the longevity of Pinwill into the 20th century ensured that his Victorian passion for a wide range of plants from peaches to trilliums carried forward to include the many new plants from plant-hunters such as Wilson and Forrest, collecting on behalf of the nurseryman Veitch of Exeter.

Magnolias at Trehane

Foxglove tree (*Paulownia*) but also towards the ground which is covered in a host of special plants. Here erythronium, trillium and dentaria flourish and the walls too are covered in a profusion of uncommon climbers including an enormous *Holboellia coriacea*.

Location: Tresillian, off A39 near Truro
Tel: (01827) 520 270
Facilities: Disabled Access, Teas, Toilets, Plant Sales, Dogs on leads, Grass Car Park.

Trelissick, Feock

Although the earliest reference to Trelissick is in 1280, it was not until the building of a new and stylish house in 1750 by John Lawrence that the grounds began to take shape. The simple two-storey villa overlooked a lawn with stands of oak, beech and Turkey oak. A walled garden had been built by the turn of the century and orchards were also present.

In the early 1800s the estate was bought by Ralph Allen Daniel whose family fortune had, like so many others of the period, been founded on tin mining. So rich was Daniel, known as "Guinea-a-minute" Daniel, that he was reputed to have been able to ride all the way to Truro without leaving his own property!

He continued planting beech and oak in the park and also planted the surrounding woodland to provide shelter for the gardens.

Thomas, his son, inheriting in 1823, extended the house and laid out miles of carriage drives. However by 1832 he was in financial difficulties and sold the estate. For over ten years the estate was neglected, until it was bought by John Davies Gilbert in 1844. His son Carew not only introduced many exotic plants, but also fruit trees with the consequence that the estate also became known as the "fruit garden of Cornwall". Surviving from this period are his smoke bush (*Cotinus coggygria*) and Chilean fire bush (*Embothrium coccineum*). Also dating from this time is the charming rustic summer house, located next to the site of the former tennis court.

It was not until 1913 when Leonard Cunliffe bought the estate that the gardens began to evolve into their present lay-out. A keen plantsman, he carried out extensive new plantings and built the solarium onto the end of the house.

His step-daughter, Ida Copeland, and her husband Ronald developed the basic character of the garden that is seen today with their plantings of rhododendrons, camellias and rare shrubs. As chairman of the family business, Spode's China, Mr Copeland took blooms from the garden direct

Sadly, by 1945 neglect had overcome most of the garden and the final death knell seemed to be the disastrous fire which completely burnt the house down in 1946. The burnt-out shell became a wilderness of bramble and sycamore, and it remained so until 1963 when the present owner, David Trehane, arrived with his large family to set about the formidable task of clearance.

Today this lovely garden has a host of delights – even the so-called weeds are beautiful – a pink haze of *Claytonia sibirica* along the drive with more everyday wild flowers such as bluebells and campions adding to the spectacle.

The first years were spent clearing, cutting and burning – leading to discoveries such as the Captain's Rock Garden and elderly trees such as crinodendron and magnolia.

Now a garden of gnarled and lively survivors has developed, interspersed with newcomers; shrubs, perennials and bulbs of every sort. Although the present owner is a camellia expert, the garden is not overwhelmed by these alone. The visitor can not only look skywards towards flowering trees such as the magnolias, pieris and styrax, and the fabulous

Hydrangeas at Trelissick

to the factory so that they could be copied accurately onto a series of beautiful plates.

Today, the first thing to greet the visitor is the wonderful view over the water of the Carrick Roads, which Hamilton described in 1897 as "blue as an Italian sky", with, "further away, Pendennis Castle surrounded in a soft blur of steel blue haze, like a big misty shadow".

Entering the garden itself, a small fig garden with eleven cultivars lies opposite the Parsley Garden formerly planted with early vegetables and herbs, now containing many fragrant and tender shrubs and climbers.

Mixed borders surround the main lawn which is dominated by a fine Japanese cedar *(Cryptomeria japonica)*.

At the entrance to the shaded walk leading to the thatched summer house, summer flowering shrubs are predominant, whilst spring bulbs mingle with wild flowers along the length of the walk.

Informal grass paths, with a wide variety of unusual rhododendrons and camellias under-planted with tiny cyclamen and erythronium, wind their way along the crest of the slope. These lead into the Dell which contains a bog garden with a wide range of moisture loving species.

A new rustic bridge leads over the sunken road to the King Harry Ferry into the most recent part of the garden, formerly an orchard, where mass plantings of daffodils and unusual shrubs are to be found.

Hydrangeas are a particular feature of this area, the National Trust having continued to plant these

species – a particular favourite of Mr Ronald Copeland. A total of approximately 150 species and cultivars have now been planted, with a particular emphasis on the more delicate 'Lacecap' varieties.

The Trust has not only continued to expand the range of plants to be found at Trelissick but has also introduced new features. An example of this is the development of a small meadow to the west of Carcadden devoted to old varieties of Cornish apples, many of which were threatened with extinction but will now be regenerated under an active programme of propagation. Here too, may be seen an example of the very rare native tree, the Plymouth pear *(Pyrus cordata)*, together with local plums from Manaccan, Kea and Portscatho. There is a 5-mile woodland walk which is open throughout the year.

Location: Off B3289 near King Harry Ferry
Tel: National Trust (01872) 862 090
Facilities: Teas, Toilets, Plant Sales, No Dogs
(except park & woodland), Car & Coach Park.

Trelowarren, Helston

There has been a settlement at Trelowarren for thousands of years. Nearby is the Halligye fougou, a well-preserved underground passage dating from the Iron Age period. The purpose of the passage remains a mystery – many theories as to its use have been put forward including storage, defence and "ritual significance".

The house itself was first referred to in the Domesday survey when it was known as Trelewarret or Treleweren, and the surrounding landscape was first enclosed in the form of a deer park in Elizabethan times.

The landscape to be seen today is for the most part an 18th-century creation, the history and philosophy of which is only now being uncovered in connection with its restoration. What is coming to light is a designed landscape of considerable size spreading from the pioneering planting of the Gweek Drive, with its rustic lodges and view points over the Helford River, to the North Drive and fir plantations of Double Lodges, all of which were laid out in the period 1752-1758 over 1500 acres. At the same time the house was refurbished by Thomas Edwards, a peripatetic architect from Greenwich, and a Pleasure Garden was laid out by Dionysus Williams. This type of garden has been described as "Rococo", a type largely destroyed by Brown and his followers and generally undertaken on a smaller scale for local polite society. A "Picturesque" landscape was also designed, including the Tremayne Quay Drive as well as the parkland approach from Garras with ponds and causeway, vernacular lodges and the Ilex Avenue.

An 18th-century plan by Dionysus Williams (CRO 22M/P/17/1) shows what must have been a very fashionable garden at this time incorporating the formal axis of the earlier geometric period and the very latest ideas in design such as serpentine walks, sites for architectural incident and of course the new idea of the ha-ha to "draw the country in". There are three main points which identify the transitional Rococo garden: small scale, ordered asymmetry and architectural incident.

These are all met at Trelowarren and will be recreated in the restoration, as well as using some of the 20th century architectural incident to give the visitor pause for thought; such as the views of the BT Earth Station on Goonhilly Downs and the wind farm at Bonython (perhaps evoking contemplation of our relentless pursuit of the new god Technology and all his attendants).

The small scale of the Rococo gardens and the rapidly evolving Natural movement led to most of these gardens being substantially altered or completely obliterated, and it is fortunate that the design was not updated at all at Trelowarren.

Ordered asymmetry, or as Batty Langley put it, "regular irregularity", is the key to the philosophic thought behind the design which arose as reaction against the artificialities of French and Dutch design. The development of this theme amongst the new wealthy Whigs and the traditional land owning class was rapid. The garden and Sir Richard Vyvyan's beautiful Rococo Chapel, which survives intact today, are a reflection of these new ideas.

Although the under-landscape remained unimproved, the 19th century saw the development of a Botanic Flower garden, located inside a walled

Trelowarren, from an engraving of 1804 by R. Polwhele

enclosure. Based on the Linnaean system of classification, it was the only known example in Cornwall. A charming "seedhouse" was built to accompany the garden, built on staddle stones to keep out vermin. This still survives adjacent to the brick walled garden.

Much work, archival and archaeological, needs to be done but four main walks have been re-established ready for the formal opening of the restoration in 1996. Good interpretative material will be available and maybe even one of William's *capriccio* garden tents will be up. Volunteers are most welcome to assist with this exciting project.

Location: Off B3293 near Helston
Tel: (01326) 221366

The main stream garden at Trengwainton

Trengwainton, Penzance

Trengwainton, from the Cornish "farm of the spring", is set at the foot of a range of granite hills to the west of Penzance.

Although there was a house here as far back as the 16th century, the present arrangement dates mainly from the beginning of the 19th century when the property was bought by Mr Rose Price whose inherited wealth enabled him to start improvements immediately. As with many other owners of large estates, his first priority was to lay out plantations surrounding the house. These were mainly stocked with ash, beech and sycamore.

He also built experimental beds within the walled garden, with sloping faces for the raising of early produce. These beds still exist and are used for a variety of plants.

Price, like many other gentry of the period, must have been a keen gardener; he also laid out a vineyard adjacent to the walled garden, the latter being shown on a map dating from 1836.

After his death his heirs were forced to sell the estate, unable to continue due to the family sugar business being affected by the Abolition of Slavery. The estate was bought in 1867 by T S Bolitho, a Cornish banker. It was not until 1925, however, when Lt.Colonel Sir Edward Bolitho inherited, that the garden began to take shape. He was assisted by three great Cornish gardeners, J C Williams of Caerhays, P D Williams of Lanarth and Canon Boscawen of Ludgvan; good friends who gave not only advice but also a large selection of rare and tender plants.

In 1926 Bolitho was offered a share in Kingdon-Ward's 1927/8 expedition to Assam and Burma, and it is from the seed obtained on the expedition that the wonderful collection of rhododendrons was raised. Many specimens bloomed here for the first time in the British Isles, including *R. macabeanum*, *R. elliottii* and *R. taggianum*.

These new species were planted out in the plantations and also in the sheltered walled gardens. The two subsequent generations of Bolithos, both dedicated and enthusiastic plantsmen, have each made a considerable contribution to the garden. As a result of this dedication down the years, Trengwainton now has a wide variety of planting.

In addition to its famous rhododendrons, the lovely stream garden has a magnificent display of pink and blue Himalayan poppies (*Meconopsis*).

The various walled gardens contain more tender plants, including a range of flowering trees, many with white flowers such as *Styrax japonica*, *Eucryphia moorei* and *Stewartia sinensis*. As a contrast to these, the surrounding borders have the astonishingly enormous echiums and the brilliant "Lobster Claw" (*Clianthus puniceus*). Other parts of the walled gardens contain sun-loving perennials and exotic climbers.

A selection of *williamsii* camellias is to be found along the Camellia Walk and beside the nearby drive are good forms of the Japanese maples (*Acer palmatum atropurpureum*) grouped with magnolias, dogwoods and rhododendrons, giving a year-round combination of colour and form.

Location: Off A394 west of Penzance
Tel: National Trust (01736) 68410 or (01736) 63021
Facilities: Disabled Access, Shop, Visitor Reception, Teas (not NT), Toilets, Dogs on Leads, Car Park.

Trerice, Newquay

For four centuries Trerice belonged to the Arundells, one of the great families of Cornwall. The house itself was rebuilt by Sir John in 1572 with a façade of Dutch-style scrolled gables overlooking a small entrance court. Originally cobbled, this has now been turfed, and earlier this century also contained some substantial trees, perhaps remnants of a formal garden. Guarding the head of the steps are the statues of the Arundell lions, two rather docile beasts originally to be found at Kenegie near Gulval, which were subsequently

Wisteria at Trerice

rescued during a road widening scheme from another Arundell property at Lifton.

To the south, where the original garden had become derelict, the National Trust has planted the grass with fruit trees, set out in a quincunx pattern, as used in the 17th century. Many Cornish varieties of apple have been planted including 'Hocking's Green' and 'Rackydown'. Amongst other fruit trees to be found here are a number of plums, 'Early Transparent', 'Denniston's Superb' and 'King of Damsons' together with 'Dutch' and 'Nottingham' medlars.

Although the walled garden at the back is almost new, the plants there have made tremendous growth. The evergreen Macartney rose (*Rosa bracteata*) which was introduced in 1795, is planted on either side of the entrance. Its large single white flowers are followed by distinctive rounded orange fruit giving colour throughout the season.

On the western boundary of the gardens are to be found a collection of olearias and elsewhere a range of buddlejas, including the unusual *B. x weyeriana* 'Golden Glow'.

In contrast to many other Cornish gardens, Trerice is essentially a summer garden, an added bonus for visitors arriving to visit the beautiful Elizabethan manor house.

A Dutch garden was originally to be found on the other side of the south wall of the Hall. Early 20th century photographs depict a formal arrangement of small beds with a few shrubs and trees in this area which was replaced some year ago by less formal borders. The white border, being the first to catch the visitor's eye, contains amongst other plants the lovely 'Iceberg' rose, *Convolvulus cneorum*, *Lavandula angustifolia* 'Nana Alba' and the white form of honesty.

In contrast, at the front of the house are the striking yellow and purple borders which include *Cotinus coggyria* 'Royal Purple', *Philadelphus coronarius* 'Aureus' and *Abutilon x suntense* 'Violetta'.

The former bowling alley, a feature which was found in many 16th and 17th century lay-outs, now contains a sundial and is flanked by mixed borders with rosemary, fuchsias and a variety of euphorbias.

Across the drive is found the parade ground – a somewhat grand term for the lawned area that was once used, not for the romantic cavaliers of the Elizabethan period, but for the Home Guard of the Second World War!

Returning towards the house via the Back Court a fine specimen of Crimson Glory vine (*Vitis coignetiae*) can be seen against the wall and also a Sydney Golden Wattle (*Acacia longifolia*) which although relatively tender, flowers profusely. Other interesting plants to be found here are *Daphne odora*

'Aureomarginata', *Schizophragma integrifolium*, and the fascinating Cruel Plant (*Araujia sericifera*), so called because the scent of the flowers attracts night-flying moths which become trapped until the flowers open again in the morning.

Last but not least, an unusual collection of lawn mowers illustrates the development of this essential piece of machinery from mid-Victorian times to the present day.

Location: Off A3058 Kestle near Newquay
Tel: National Trust (01637) 875 404
Facilities: Disabled Access, Tea room and shop, Toilets, Plant Sales, No Dogs, Car & Coach Park, Lawnmower Museum.

Tresco Abbey Gardens, Isles of Scilly

Few people visiting Tresco today and being overwhelmed by its cornucopia of riches, can imagine the bare and exposed nature of the island before the development of the garden.

In 1834, the vegetation did not exceed anything more prominent than heather and bracken with a few scrubby sycamore and willow scattered here and there.

It was at this time that Augustus Smith took up residence on the island in the position of Lord Proprietor. Amongst the granite rocks he found the ruins of Tresco Abbey and it was round this ruin that he laid out a small formal garden.

As time progressed he laid out terraces and walks, vistas and avenues, fishponds and rockeries, in all amounting to an amazing 17 acres.

A keen collector of seeds, particularly from the southern hemisphere, he planted the garden with an immense variety of sub-tropical plants which flourished in the equable maritime climate.

Essential also were shelter trees, which by the time Augustus died in 1872 had only reached 15-18 feet in height.

In addition to planting many succulents and other exotics, he also developed an ornamental wildfowl area on the grass sloping towards the Abbey Pool and carried out the initial planting of the Long Walk.

Following on from Augustus, Thomas Algernon Dorrien-Smith (particularly remembered for his development of the bulb industry) instigated the major windbreak, carefully selecting Monterey pine and cypress. He also, naturally, continued planting within his predecessor's framework.

From the end of the First World War, his son Major Arthur was instrumental in introducing

The tropical garden at Tresco

many more plants; particularly those he had himself discovered in the Chatham Islands and New Zealand.

The subsequent Dorrien-Smiths, Thomas and Robert, continued the fine tradition with the result that Tresco has become one of the most exciting gardens, not only in Great Britain but throughout the world.

The garden itself is centred on the old ruins of the Abbey now festooned with climbing plants and wall succulents. Dominant on the walls are the succulent rosettes of aeonium species – one of the garden's most famous features.

Ginger lilies (*Hedychiums*) and bananas thrive here without protection as does the lemon *(Citrus limon)* the latter rarely without fruit.

The well garden is the site where Augustus planted the first plant, an *Agave americana*. This area still contains many similar plants which are more normally seen growing under glass.

On leaving the Well garden, the vast West Rockery rises upwards encrusted with plants including vivid mesembryanthemums, architectural agaves and, at its base, a series of pools with such

tender rarities as the 'Chatham Island' Forget-Me-Not (*Myosotidium hortensia*) with its giant blue flowers and substantial leaves.

The Middle Terrace, crossing the garden from east to west, specialises in sun-lovers where amazing plants such as *Puya alpestris* with its waxy green flowers can be found. The brilliant blooms of perennial "ice plants" festoon the rocks and scented pelargoniums scramble amongst them.

A summerhouse roofed with Burmese honeysuckle (*Lonicera hildebrandtiana*) overlooks a small pool with wide borders on either side. The unbelievable tree echiums also flourish in this area of the garden, hybridization having produced a wide range of colour forms.

South African plants are also a feature of the gardens, with the collection of proteas being the most northerly in the world.

From the Protea Walk the view from the Top Terrace including "Father Neptune" (an old figurehead) is probably Tresco's most famous vista, with glimpses of the sea through enormous palm trees and the amazing red-flowered metrosideros.

Although space precludes further description, there are many other areas of the garden full of exotic and tender treasures.

As a footnote, the visitor should be aware that the amazing plants in the garden continue to flourish in spite of two severe climatic episodes. During the first, sub-zero temperatures and freezing winds caused loss and damage on a scale never previously thought possible. This was followed closely by the great storm of 1990 when the shelter belt was severely damaged, losing over 400 mature trees in one day! Notwithstanding, the gardens of Tresco have risen phoenix-like from the devastation, with the new shelter-belts growing rapidly and the exotic gardens returning to their former glory.

Location: Isles of Scilly, by boat or helicopter from Penzance.
Tel: (01720) 422 849 or 422 868
Facilities: Disabled Access, Teas (Feb to Nov), Toilets, Plant Sales, Dogs on leads.

Trevarno Manor Gardens, Helston

Trevarno lies hidden in a small valley just to the north of Helston and it was not until the early 1800s that gardening began here. In 1838 Christopher Wallis Popham, grandson of Christopher Wallis, built the walled kitchen garden, its greenhouses and the lake. From these beginnings, it was left to the subsequent owner, William Bickford-Smith, to expand both the planting and ornamental features.

Arriving in 1874, he embarked on grandiose schemes including an impressive Rock Garden with its series of mounds intersected by winding paths and steps. A small grotto was included with shelves to hold candles to reflect the dripping water.

Nearer the house, an Italian garden originally containing formal rose beds and statuary was constructed at the far end of the main lawn. The lake was then extended, a formal terrace running along its length with a pretty neo-Gothic boathouse at one end.

Extensive planting was also carried out from this period, and was continued by successive generations of the same family. Many fine specimen trees are to be found including swamp cypress (*Taxodium distichum*) on the island in the lake and a substantial collection of rhododendrons, azaleas and acers, many to be found as an understorey to mature beech and oak woodland. More recent planting has included rare and tender conifers such as Kashmir cypress (*Cupressus himalanica var. darjeelingensis*) near the rockery and *Dacrydium franklinii* in the Pinetum.

The lake at Trevarno

Although the walled gardens and greenhouses have been neglected until recently, the new owners have initiated a programme of restoration.

The vinery, housing Muscat and Black Hamburgh grapevines dating from the turn of the century, is to be renovated and the lower walled garden is to become a herb garden with a wide variety of medicinal and culinary herbs.

In addition to the gardens, the lower pools and leats will also be cleared as part of an exciting project involving the restoration of the mill further downstream. Visitors will be able to park at the proposed Visitor and Craft Centre at the main house and wander through the lovely gardens following the stream down to the mill.

Location: Off B3302 west of Helston
Tel: (01326) 574274
Facilities: Part Disabled Access, Teas, Toilets, Dogs on leads, Car & Coach Park.

Trewidden, Penzance

Trewidden is set in the hills two miles west of Penzance, the house and gardens situated at the end of a drive half a mile long running from the Penzance-Land's End road. As it faces south and south-west, on the "toe" of the Cornish peninsula, full use has been made of the climatic situation which enables many plants which are normally tender on the mainland to be successfully cultivated.

The gardens were started in 1880 by Mr T.B. Bolitho and his daughter, Mary, who on her marriage became Mrs Charles Williams. She and her husband also lived at Greenway, Churston Ferrers, Devon, and Caerhays Castle, Cornwall, both houses with great gardens, but it was at Trewidden that Mrs Williams continued planting until her death in 1977. *Camellia reticulata* 'Mary Williams' was named after her.

The original gardens, which covered about 25 acres, included a walled kitchen garden of one and a half acres, facing south, for the growing of vegetables for the house. Numerous glasshouses, boiler houses and frames were built to produce even earlier crops such as tomatoes, peaches and melons. An old Cornish open-cast tin mine nearby provided an excellent location for tree ferns, the spoil heaps being known as "the Burrows" (the name normally given to mine waste in Cornwall). A small rock garden with a pond and waterfall was also incorporated into this area. Shelter belts of griselinia, pines and evergreen oaks were planted on windward sides of the garden, and paths were laid out and edged with rocks taken from the tin mine.

A large pond was dug out and fountains installed, and a ha-ha with a commanding view of

The lake at Trewidden in the late 19th century

the Lizard Peninsula across Mount's Bay separated the terrace from fields on the north-east side of the house. Up to 15 gardeners were employed at Trewidden during to first half of the century to deal with this extensive garden.

Of the original plantings the following remain today: Chilean hazel (*Gevuina avellana*), tree ferns, *Magnolia veitchii* (which is probably the largest in the country), Manglietia, *Lithocarpus butia*, *Cinnamonum* and *Magnolia campbellii*. *Manglietia insignis*, of the magnolia family, was planted in 1893. In 1911 this was the first one of its kind to flower in this country and it continues to be a magnificent sight when in flower every year. (Both the *Gevuina* and *Magnolia obovata* are pictured in Thurston's book "British and Foreign Trees and Shrubs in Cornwall", published in 1930.)

Recent years, notably 1987 and 1990, saw the destruction of many trees. In the cold winter of 1987 all of the griselinia were killed outright; these had formed the basis of windbreaks and were 40 to 50 feet high. Also killed were White Alder (*Clethra delavayii*), Ribbon Wood (*Plagianthus regius*) and *Magnolia nitida*. Luckily, 18 inches of snow protected the base of some shrubs and, although being damaged down to this level, they have since sprouted again. The severe gales of 1990 brought down 50 large trees onto shrubs and buildings; an additional 150 trees came down in the shelter-belts.

Following these two disasters, an ongoing programme of replanting has been taking place. Hundreds of trees of hardier genera have been planted, for example pines, hollies, evergreen oaks, laurel and sycamores. New shrub planting has been carried out, too: rhododendrons, camellias, (now over 300 different cultivars) and azaleas, among others. Some camellias, magnolias, rhododendrons and tree ferns seed themselves freely, whilst other have to be propagated vegetatively. The pond has been renovated and extended, and an island formed in it. It is fed by surplus clean rainwater from the roofs of nearby buildings. The walled garden and glasshouses are now used for the raising of plants for sale (camellias being propagated for wholesale trade) and for future plantings within the gardens.

Location: West of Penzance
Tel: (01736) 63106 or 62087
NB: The house and garden area with ha-ha are not open to the public.
Facilities: Disabled Access, Toilets, Plant Sales (not Sundays), Dogs on leads, Car Park.

Trewithen Gardens, Grampound Road

Trewithen, covering some thirty acres, is situated on the outskirts of the village of Probus, famous for its impressive parish church.

The house and parkland were first laid out by Philip Hawkins at the beginning of the 18th century. Further planting was carried out by his successor Thomas, who was particularly interested in growing trees, producing a pamphlet in detailing their growth.

A plan dating from the middle of the 18th century shows the extensive plantations surrounding the house, with vistas, a labyrinth and what appear to be bastions overlooking the countryside.

Following the death of Thomas in 1766, the estate remained relatively untouched until the arrival of George Johnstone at the beginning of this century. George Johnstone was an accomplished plantsman and author of "Asiatic Magnolias in Cultivation" in 1955.

When Johnstone inherited, it was necessary to carry out a great deal of clearance; the house had become overwhelmed by surrounding woodland.

The walled garden (the original herb garden, contemporary with the house) was still a drying area for the laundry. This was transformed with formal paths (made of granite setts from the Redruth tramway), a pergola and a delightful corner summerhouse.

Today, looking beyond the wall of the garden, a great bank of *Pieris formosa var. forrestii* looms upward, with spectacular young foliage and flowers.

Pool sculpture in the walled garden at Trewithen

Trewithen

The house overlooks the main lawn – stretching for over 200 metres, it is lined on both sides by a remarkable range of trees and shrubs including a superb *Magnolia campbellii spp. mollicomata*, introduced from China by George Forrest.

To each side of the lawn are many glades amongst the trees; these are rich with many rare shrubs and small trees such as *Rehderodendron macrocarpum* and various acers.

A mossy bank covered in cyclamen leads onwards to the camellia walk where there are camellia varieties named after the owners at Trewithen, 'Elizabeth Johnstone' and 'Trewithen Pink', can be found amongst a large and varied collection of camellias.

At the end of the walk, the now disused Cock Pit shelters tree ferns and a delicate pink form of *Magnolia sprengeri*.

A path leads out from the Cock Pit into newer plantings where a varied collection of pittosporum is displayed.

Between the Cock Pit and the house is an area that was extensively damaged during the 1990 storm. Although many fine eucryphias up to 70ft in

The stream at Trewoofe

height were blown down, one remains as a reminder of past glories. All is not gloom, however, as the spaces created by the loss of large trees have been used for new plantings.

Towards the house are further groves of beautiful magnolias and rhododendrons, one of the garden's most famous plants being a magnificent specimen of *Rhododendron macabeanum* with enormous trusses of yellow flowers. A number of fine rhododendron hybrids have been raised at the garden – R. 'Alison Johnstone' and 'Jack Skilton' being two of them.

Location: East of Probus on A390
Tel: (01726) 883 647
Facilities: Disabled Access, Teas, Toilets, Plant Sales, Dogs on leads, Car & Coach Park.

Trewoofe House, Lamorna

Trewoofe is one of the most remote gardens in the country, at the head of the Lamorna valley in the "Far West".

The painter Charles Napper and his wife Ella, who was a jeweller and potter, came to join the Lamorna artistic community in 1913, building a cottage and studio on land consisting of three small Cornish meadows which had a mill leat running through to feed the ancient Clappen Mill. Charles and Ella made a garden around the house and enlarged the leat to form a trout pond. Lamorna Birch painted a major work of it in 1938 entitled "Ella's Garden".

The existing garden is, however, the product of the descendants of Charles Napper and is full of interesting plants and colour combinations created over the last 20 years. Tons of rock have been moved around to create a series of rockeries where a wide variety of plants survive despite the wind. The owner has had to modify her planting ambitions because of the climate and is establishing a wide range of hardy perennials. Part of the mill leat is now a fine bog garden.

Location: Off B3315 west of Penzance
Tel: (01736) 810 269
Facilities: Part Disabled Access, Teas, Plant Sales, Toilets, No Dogs, Limited Car Parking.

Truro, Victoria Gardens

Opened in 1898, these public gardens were designed in the typical style of the period, containing a bandstand, ornate public shelter and fountain, the latter having been moved from its former position in the centre of Boscawen Street.

The gardens, only two minutes walk from the city centre, provide a perfect setting for many splendid specimen trees including majestic weeping elms and beech. Shrubberies and herbaceous borders are supplemented by colourful annual bedding. These make a backdrop for the summer concerts and children's entertainments which provide continuous usage of the park, thus avoiding the decay which has affected so many other Victorian parks.

A unique feature of the gardens is the method by which water is fed to the fountain, fishpond and waterfall. This is by means of a hydraulic ram situated in the old mill leat, the leat having begun its course at the weir located at the bottom of the gardens.

Although many years have passed since the park keeper, Mr Treweek, rang a large bell and shouted "All out, all out", the city councillors still retain the bell and have plans to use it during their proposed centenary celebrations in 1998.

Location: Town centre, Truro

Truro, Boscawen Park

The city council also maintains Boscawen Park, a complete contrast to the slopes and amphitheatre style of Victoria Gardens. It is a very flat area almost at water level and by the side of what used to be a thriving port. The historic interest at the park is the building now known as Trennick Mill Restaurant, on the opposite side of Malpas Road and adjacent to the duck pond, once a mill house constructed between 1750 and 1800. The mill was powered by water which was probably delivered by a wooden chute from a higher point up the valley. The watercourse continued on a line to the other side of the saltings and discharged onto the mud flats. This form of power was presumably unsuccessful, as a steam engine was installed in 1809.

In 1911 Boscawen Park Lodge was formerly known as the Mill Junket House. In later years it was used as tea rooms, then as accommodation for members of Parks staff, and has now reverted to restaurant use.

The duck pond or "Swan Pool" is one of the most popular areas of the park, being visited all the year round by both children and adults, feeding the abundant population of wild fowl. Across Malpas Road from the duck pond are sports pitches.

Part of the park was built on top of a former rubbish tip located on the mud flats. Shortly after

F W Meyer's plan of 1895 for Boscawen Park, Truro

World War II the sports field was developed and at a later date formal bedding and planted areas created as seen in the present day.

Interestingly, proposals for the development of the park were made as early as 1895 when F W Meyer of the famous Veitch nurseries at Exeter produced a plan for a public park which included playing fields, a lodge, bandstand and various planted areas ranging from sub-tropical areas through to herbaceous and rhododendron plantings. He also showed an area of gravel beach at the Malpas end of the park and a large pool which was presumably to be fed by the existing supply from the mill leat.

Location: Off Malpas Road, Truro

Watergate Garden, Trelill, Nr. Bodmin

Watergate Garden was originally a small cottage garden with arches of rambler roses, daffodils, bluebells and a few shrubs and trees, its boundary formed by a fast running stream which joins the river Allen below. The house was two old miners' cottages, joined and extended to make one house.

The wisteria, which was planted to grow up the front of the house, is now very large, covering the whole front and flowers freely in May.

In 1952 the then owner, Captain John Hicks R.N., purchased an acre of land on the far side of the stream, thus extending the garden to about 3 acres and creating a very attractive setting with stream and woods as a background. Bluebells and daffodils, including some unusual cultivars, abound. Captain Hicks planted magnolias, rhododendrons and camellias, which are now large mature trees and shrubs.

In 1974 Lt.Colonel and Mrs Guy Browne bought Watergate and continued to plant and cultivate this garden. Some new features have been introduced such as a large herbaceous border, a bog garden and primula garden alongside the stream. Some fairly unusual candelabra primulas such as 'Inverewe', 'Rowallane Rose' and 'poissonii' can be seen in the late spring.

The far end of the garden contains a very large weeping lime tree, a vegetable garden and small orchard with an apiary beyond.

Location: Trelill, Nr. Bodmin on the St Teath road from Trelill (opposite Pengenna Farm).
Tel: (01208) 850 712
Facilities: Part Disabled Access, Teas, Toilets, Plant Sales, Dogs on leads.
N.B. No parking facilities other than along the road.

A brilliant acer at Woodland Garden

Woodland Garden, Helston

Woodland Garden is two and a half acres of a small valley about four miles south of Helston and almost in the centre of the Lizard Peninsula. The hamlet in which it is situated, Bojorrow, was mentioned in the Doomsday Book, its numbers of sheep and cows being compared with those of Trelowarren. Very much older than the settlement are the rocks lying below. The dense white igneous boulders of the Meneage crush zone which lie on and just under the land are of quartzite and some are, as can be seen, quite a size.

R M Barton's "Introduction to the Geology of Cornwall" says that pillow lava rocks, found in only a few locations "have no equivalent elsewhere in Britain" and have "caused much speculation since the early days of geological research in the county". The pillow lava is alkaline, but that does not prevent the owners from growing all manner of calcifuge plants without problems.

The valley runs from east to west creating a funnel for the prevailing south-westerly winds from Mount's Bay, which is only about 2 miles away. Although the garden may feel warm and sheltered most of the year, growing is not as easy as it may seem. Gales from the west easily get through such defences as have so far managed to grow. Although the garden is better protected on the east, it is the winter winds from this direction that do most damage.

The soil is very heavy clay, making for hard work! Climatic conditions are good, with annual rainfall of about 50 inches; hard frosts are rare and the mean temperature in January is over 6 degrees C. The biggest problem is late spring frosts, consequently quite hardy plants look miserable after losing young growths and flowers.

The garden is informal and has been developed since about 1978, with many varieties of camellia, rhododendron and magnolia, some of which are now achieving major size and thriving. Specimens such as *Magnolia soulangeana* 'Picture' and *M. soulangeana* 'Rubra', Canary Island pine (*Pinus canariensis*), Kashmir cypress (*Cupressus var. himalanica darjeelingensis*) and Chilean fire bush (*Embothrium coccineum*) are on the way to being good specimens. Exotic plants from many parts of the world are also to be found here – originally acquired as mother plants for the nursery. Since the owners stopped propagating young plants, they have opened up the valley with improved paths and plan to leave it all as natural and "wild" as possible.

Visitors are welcome to picnic or spend the whole afternoon here, taking time to observe the wild life as well as the garden. A heron regularly sweeps up the stream trying to catch the trout (having had all the goldfish in the pond) and buzzards are almost always wheeling high, just to the south-west.

About a quarter of a mile up the road beyond the ford are Goonhilly Downs, a vast open area with extensive views across the peninsula. Visitors can walk to the downs along the lane and as far over it as desired, taking dogs if wished. It is designated a Site of Special Scientific Interest and natural nature reserve, with fine ericas present, especially the Cornish heath (*Erica vagans*).

Location: Garras, Helston – off B3293 Lizard road
Tel: (01326) 221 295
Facilities: No Disabled Access, Plant Sales, No Dogs, Car Park. N.B. Dogs on leads permitted on downs.

Bibliography and Further Reading

ALLOM, T. (1831). *Cornwall Illustrated in a Series of Views...* with Historical and Descriptive Accounts by J Britton and E W Brayley

BISGROVE, Richard (1990). *The English Garden.* Penguin.

CORNISH GARDEN SOCIETY, journal of: *The Cornish Garden*

BORLASE, W. (1758). *The Natural History of Cornwall.* Oxford. (1754) *The Antiquities of Cornwall* Reprinted 1973.

CAREW, R. (1602). *The Survey of Cornwall* ed. F E Halliday, with the maps of John Norden, repr. 1969

CORNISH ARCHAEOLOGICAL SOCIETY, Journal of: *Cornish Archaeology.*

DAUBENY, C.G.B. (1864). Tresco, Scilly Islands, and Mr Robert Fox's gardens at Grove Hill and Penjerrick near Falmouth. List of tender plants. J.R.I.C. 1(1): 71-73.

DAVEY, F.H. (1897). Acclimatisation of exotics in Cornwall, Falmouth-Truro district, J. Roy. Inst. Cornwall 13: 313-343 [Lists plants from Burncoose, Carclew, Enys, Grove Hill, Menabilly, Porthgwidden, Rosehill, Trelissick and Tremough.]

DOBLE, G.H. (1923-44). *Cornish Saints.*

DOMESDAY (1086). *Domesday Book:* 10. Cornwall, repr. Chichester, 1979.

FIENNES, C. (1699). *Through England on a Side Saddle.* See *Early Tours* (1969)

GILBERT, C.S. (1820). *Historical Survey of Cornwall*, vol. 2.

GILBERT, D. (1838) *Parochial History of Cornwall, founded on the manuscript histories of Mr Hals and Mr Tonkin*, 4 vols.

GILL, C. (1995) *The Great Cornish Families*

HALLIDAY, F.C. *A History of Cornwall*

HENDERSON, Charles. (1935) *Essays in Cornish History.* – Henderson MSS in R.I.C.

HITCHINS, F. (1824) *The History of Cornwall*, 2 vols. compiled by Fortescue Hitchins and edited by Samuel Drew, Helston.

HUNT, David & PETT, Douglas (1991). *Historic Gardens in Cornwall*

LAKE (1867-72) *Lake's Parochial History of the County of Cornwall*, Polsue, J. 4 vols., Truro. Repr. Wakefield, 1974.

LAWMAN, J. (1994) – *A Natural History of the Lizard Peninsula.*

LOUDON, J.C. (1822). *Encyclopaedia of Horticulture.*

LYSONS, D. & S. (1814). *Magna Britannia...* volume the third, Cornwall.

McCABE, H. (1988). *Houses and Gardens of Cornwall.* Padstow.

McLEAN, Teresa. *Medieval English Gardens*

MATON, W.G. (1794). *Observations on the Western Counties of England.*

MITCHELL, HALLET & WHITE (1990). *Champion Trees in the British Isles* – Forestry Commission

OLD CORNWALL. The Journal of the Federation of Old Cornwall Societies.

PEVSNER, N. (1970). *The Buildings of England.* 2nd ed., revised by Enid Radcliffe.

POLWHELE, R. (1803) *The History of Cornwall.*

REDDING, C. (1842). *An Illustrated Itinerary of the County of Cornwall.*

Royal Institution of Cornwall, Journal of (1864-)

ROWSE, A.L. (1937) *Sir Richard Grenville.* (1941) *Tudor Cornwall.*

STOCKDALE, F.W.L. (1824). *A Tour to the West of England.* See *Early Tours* (1967).

STROUD, D. (1962) *Humphry Repton.*

THURSTON, E. (1930). *British and Foreign Trees and Shrubs in Cornwall.* Published for the Royal Institution of Cornwall by Cambridge University Press, Cambridge.

TWYCROSS, E. (1846). *The Mansions of England and Wales. County of Cornwall.*

Index